Mental Health Today And Tomorrow

Exploring current and future trends in mental health

Edited by
David Crepaz-Keay

CW00524012

mental
health
foundation

Pavilion

Mental Health Today... And Tomorrow

Exploring current and future trends in mental health

© David Crepaz-Keay 2015

The authors have asserted their rights in accordance with the Copyright, Designs and Patents Act (1988) to be identified as the authors of this work.

Published by:
Pavilion Publishing and Media Ltd
Rayford House
School Road
Hove
East Sussex
BN3 5HX
Tel: 01273 434 943
Fax: 01273 227 308
Email: info@pavpub.com

Published 2015

A catalogue record for this book is available from the British Library.

ISBN: 978-1-910366-33-2

Pavilion is the leading training and development provider and publisher in the health, social care and allied fields, providing a range of innovative training solutions underpinned by sound research and professional values. We aim to put our customers first, through excellent customer service and value.

Edited by: David Crepaz-Keay
Production editor: Mike Benge, Pavilion Publishing and Media Ltd
Cover design: Emma Dawe, Pavilion Publishing and Media Ltd
Page layout and typesetting: Emma Dawe, Pavilion Publishing and Media Ltd
Printing: CMP Digital Print Solutions

Contents

Contributors

Dr David Crepaz-Keay

Dr David Crepaz-Keay is Head of Empowerment and Social Inclusion at the Mental Health Foundation and has led the development, delivery and evaluation of 65 self-management courses for people with a severe psychiatric diagnosis across England and Wales, helped ensure effective involvement of mental health service users in the development of *Together for Mental Health: A cross-government strategy for mental health and wellbeing in Wales*, and is part of a working group developing impact assessment tools for the strategy. He has been a technical adviser to the World Health Organization on empowerment issues, chaired a WHO working group on developing indicators of involvement, and has spoken and written widely on involvement, empowerment, self-management and peer support.

David is an eloquent and passionate campaigner against discrimination on the grounds of mental health history. With over 25 years of involvement, first as a user of mental health services and later as a campaigner, he is also an advocate of service user voices being included in mental health service planning and delivery.

David was a Commissioner for Patient and Public Involvement in Health (January 2003 – August 2007). The commission (CPPIH) was created to give the public a voice in decisions that affect their health. He was a founder member of the English national survivor user network (NSUN).

Before working in mental health, David wrote economic models at HM Treasury and models of underground water systems for the water industry. He is also a qualified cricket umpire.

Anne Beales MBE

Anne Beales is Director of Service User Involvement at Together: For Mental Wellbeing, a mental health charity and service provider. She has over 16 years' experience working directly with those who access mental health services. In 2008 until 2014, Anne was appointed as one of just two service user consultants to the NHS Confederation Mental Health Network (MHN) and she served as part of the government Social Work Task Force, set up to examine the quality, recruitment and retention of the profession. Anne also sits on the Equalities Ministerial Advisory Group for Mental Health, has been appointed as a Trustee for Disability Rights UK and has recently been appointed to sit on the advisory board for Healthwatch England's public enquiry into unsafe discharge.

She received an MBE for services to healthcare for her role setting up the Capital Project Trust, and was a founding member of NSUN, which she continues to support.

Andy Bell

Andy Bell is Deputy Chief Executive at Centre for Mental Health, an independent charity seeking a fairer chance in life for people with mental health problems. Andy began at the centre in 2002 before which he worked at The King's Fund. Andy is also a trustee of YoungMinds, the children and young people's mental health charity.

Mark Brown

Mark Brown is Development Director of the social enterprise Social Spider CIC. He founded and edited *One in Four* between 2006 and 2014, a national mental health magazine written by and for people with mental health difficulties. Increasingly, Mark focuses on mental health and social and digital innovation. In 2014 he was recognised by *Health Service Journal* and *Nursing Times* as a 'Social Media Pioneer'. In 2014, with funding from Public Health England, he launched *A Day in the Life*, a crowd-sourced blogging project to create a snapshot of life in England as lived by people with mental health difficulties.

Eva Cyhlarova

Dr Eva Cyhlarova is an independent researcher working in health and social care and specialising in mental health. She is a Research Associate of the Centre for Mental Health, London, and Visiting Academic at the Department of Physiology, Anatomy and Genetics, University of Oxford. For the last five years she was the Head of Research at the Mental Health Foundation, managing a portfolio of research projects across mental health, learning disabilities and dementia. Following a DPhil in Experimental Psychology at the University of Oxford, she worked as a Senior Research Scientist at the Department of Physiology, Anatomy and Genetics at Oxford, managing a number of large-scale projects on neurodevelopmental disorders. She also worked as a Senior Medical Writer and an Account Manager in a Medical Communications Agency. Eva also holds a master's degree in psychosocial sciences and a bachelor's degree in philosophy and religion. Her research interests include service improvement, user-led approaches, self-management and services user involvement.

Isabella Goldie

Isabella Goldie is the Director of Delivery and Development for the Mental Health Foundation, and from 2005 to 2014 was Head of Scotland for the organisation. Isabella oversaw the merger of the Foundation with the Scottish Development Centre for Mental Health and is responsible for leading the 10-year Review of Mental Health Services for the Scottish Government. Previous appointments include 12 years of voluntary sector service experience within Glasgow Association for Mental Health (GAMH) in a range of posts, and during this period Isabella sat as an invited member on the International Centre for Clubhouse Development Faculty Board.

She has a master's degree in Public Mental Health from the University of Glasgow and trained and worked as a registered mental health nurse (RMN) for nine years within NHS Greater Glasgow and Clyde.

Jolie Goodman

Jolie combines her artistic work with a career in the mental health sector. Her work in mental health has been rooted in her personal desire to bring about change and improvement in the services that people receive. She has over a decade of experience as a group facilitator and is currently working part time for the Mental Health Foundation as Manager and Lead Facilitator of the project Later Life Self-help Groups in Extra Care/Retirement Housing. As an artist Jolie makes a variety of work examples of which can be seen on her website: www.joliegoodman.co.uk. She paints portraits for commissions and makes illustrations for organisations including the Lancet Psychiatry.

Naomi James

Naomi James is the Research and Regional Development Manager for NSUN where her main role is to strengthen the direct political voice of people with experience of trauma and distress, reviewing mental health policy and influencing the development of mental health services. Naomi is involved with several research projects involving England-wide co-ordination of people and groups to improve emotional well-being. Naomi's work has also involved managing the National Involvement Partnership, and she gave evidence to the parliamentary health select committee for the post-legislative scrutiny and review of the 2007 amendments to the Mental Health Act (2013).

Passionate about improving inclusive practices in research and for mobilising communities, Naomi's ongoing study investigates the practice of Participatory Video for Mental Health. Naomi has a background in the arts with a BA in Fine Art and an MA in Glass and Video Production.

Paula Lavis BA Hons, BSc Hons, Dip Inf.

Paula has worked in the children and young people's mental health sector for about 15 years. Most of her experience is from working in the voluntary sector in a policy development role, but she has also worked in government and for professional bodies. She has a background in psychology, and is currently the Co-ordinator and Policy Lead for the Children and Young People's Mental Health Coalition.

Simon Lawton-Smith

Simon Lawton-Smith was Head of Policy at the Mental Health Foundation from 2008 to 2013. Between 2003 and 2008 he was Senior Fellow in Mental Health at The King's Fund, where he led the mental health work programme, linking policy development with service development and research projects. From 1997 to 2003 he was Head of Public Affairs at national service provider mental health charity Together. He is author/co-author of a range of reports and articles on mental health issues and has been chair of the anti-stigma mental health charity ok2b. From 1979 to 1997 Simon worked on a range of policy issues in the civil service, at the Department of Health, the Northern Ireland Office and the Cabinet Office.

Lily Makurah Bsc (hons) PGdip MPH

A National Programme Manager in Public Health England's Public Mental Health Team, Lily has wide experience of public health policy planning, delivery and implementation gained over 20 years of working in local authorities, Department of Health, NHS and NGOs. Lily's experience at both national and local level in the northwest, northeast, the south of England and London has had an emphasis on improving outcomes for children and young people as a high priority. Lily's Public Health England role has a particular focus on mental health promotion and the prevention of mental illness. Her work to secure improvements in public mental health across England includes partnerships with NHS England, local government, third sector and other key stakeholders.

Barbara McIntosh

Barbara has worked across children, family and adult services in the NHS, social services and the voluntary sector, focusing on mental health, learning disability and long-term conditions. She has a particular interest in prevention and early intervention in children's mental health. She was a Director and National Head of Children's Programmes over a 10-year period at the Mental Health Foundation. Barbara previously worked at The King's Fund and London University.

Barbara is currently a Director of Health Watch Sutton, a Non Executive Director at Swanton Care and a Trustee at Hft and the Richard James Trust.

She has a BA in Anthropology and Social Work from McMaster University in Canada and an MSc in Health and Social Policy from the London School of Economics.

Chris O'Sullivan

Chris led SUPPORT at the Scottish Development Centre (SDC), an EU Public Health Programme Project providing policy and research support to the European Commission in developing and implementing an EU-wide approach to public mental health. Before joining SDC in 2006, Chris worked for 'see me', Scotland's national anti-stigma campaign, and until December 2012 he served as Chair of Trustees for Action on Depression. Chris leads the Policy and Development team in Scotland, which works with a range of partners to support capacity building for mental health, and to raise awareness of mental health. The team works locally, nationally and internationally to ensure that practice and policy reflect the best available evidence and include lived experience wherever possible.

Chris is currently working with the Scottish Government on a major technology project to support people to self-manage distress. In 2011 Chris was selected as a founding member of the Royal Society of Edinburgh Young Academy of Scotland.

Emma Perry

Emma Perry is a researcher with a background in criminal justice, education and mental health. Her PhD provided a critique of cognitive-behavioural rehabilitation programmes run by the probation service. She has written articles on the construction of gender and class in criminal justice settings and has co-authored a review of the social class gap in educational achievement for the Royal Society of Arts. She is also an editorial board member of the *Journal of Gender Studies*.

Emma is currently Research Project Co-ordinator at NSUN where her work has focused on service user involvement in mental health commissioning. She has written a review of values-based commissioning in the West Midlands and worked with Mind to produce an accessible guide to commissioning for service users. In addition to her work on the language of mental health, Emma has also written an overview of service user involvement in health and social care policy as part of the National Involvement Partnership project.

Claire Robson

Claire Robson works as a senior public health specialist, leading on improving public health outcomes for school aged children within Public Health England's Children, Young People and Families team. Claire has over 20 years' experience in health improvement policy and practice spanning children and young people, workplace and education settings, tobacco control and mental health. Claire holds a master's degree in Health Promotion and is currently working towards registration with the Faculty of Public Health as a Public Health Consultant.

Sarah Stewart-Brown BM BCh, PhD FFPH

Sarah Stewart-Brown is Professor of Public Health at Warwick Medical School, University of Warwick. Her research interests focus on public mental health and child public health, and she led the development of the Warwick-Edinburgh Mental Well-being Scale, which has played a key role in the development of policy and practice in public mental health.

Sarah chairs Public Health England's Expert Advisory Group on Mental Health and Wellbeing, is Vice Chair of the Public Health England Mental Health and Wellbeing Corporate Board, and sits on the Public Health England Corporate Board on Reducing Disease and Disability and the Ministerial Advisory Committee implementing the English Strategy 'No Health Without Mental Health'. She advises both the Scottish and Welsh governments on public mental health in a variety of contexts. She is Chair of the UK Faculty of Public Health's Mental Health Committee.

Sarah has published extensively and holds a Doctor of Philosophy Degree from Bristol University and is a Fellow of the UK Faculty of Public Health, Royal College of Physicians of London, and the UK Royal College of Paediatrics and Child Health.

Toby Williamson

Toby joined the Mental Health Foundation in 2002 as Head of Development and Later Life where he is responsible for the Foundation's mental health in later life and dementia programme, as well as leading on its mental capacity work. This has included qualitative and quantitative research, mental capacity best interests decisions, values in mental health and service development projects in a wide range of areas.

Toby has led on policy work at the foundation and for 18 months was seconded to work at the Ministry of Justice on their Mental Capacity Act Implementation Programme. He has previously worked and managed adult mental health services where he was involved in setting up and managing a variety of services for people with severe and enduring mental health problems living in the community.

Toby has a BA (Hons) in Social Administration and Sociology (Bristol University), a Postgraduate Diploma in Mental Health Innovations (LSE) and a Postgraduate Diploma in Care Policy and Management (London Metropolitan),

Emily Wooster

Emily has worked in the not-for-profit sector for 14 years with particular expertise in mental health policy analysis, having worked for both Mind and the Mental Health Foundation. She has had numerous publications in magazines and academic journals, and has provided training and capacity building in the UK and overseas in participatory approaches to social research and campaigning. Emily has recently taken up the post of Head of Development for Wales for the Mental Health Foundation, having led on their policy work before that.

Introduction

Mental health is starting to attract the broader attention it needs and deserves. For far too long it has been the poor relation of physical health, despite the now obvious truth of the World Health Organization's 'No health without mental health', a key phrase that helped launch their comprehensive mental health action plan, and which was subsequently adopted as the title of the current UK mental health policy. This book marks a turning point in UK mental health theory, policy and practice. Mental health services have spent most of their history cut off from the rest of society, largely performing the job of picking up the pieces after everything else has failed. Its role and purpose needs to change, and the less than splendid isolation is coming to an end.

This change is happening in a number of places. Well-being is no longer seen as a fluffy middle class concept, but as a fundamental part of the human condition. The happiness agenda may have come and gone, but well-being and public mental health seem likely to stay rather longer. Mental well-being is now considered by an increasing number of people as both a measurable and a possible outcome of well-designed interventions. But understanding and definitions of well-being are not consistent, and the overlap with public mental health and preventing mental ill-health can be confusing. We hope some of the chapters dedicated to these themes will shed some light and help people to develop their own ideas.

The nature of public mental health itself is also changing. The complicated relationship between mental health and mental ill-health is becoming more widely accepted and explored although perhaps not completely understood. Public mental health is now a legitimate lens through which to understand our responses to everything from prevention to mental health service provision. This can be challenging as the term 'mental health' and the provision of what have always been referred to as mental health services almost always refers to mental illness services and treatment delivery. We need to get used to saying 'mental health' when we mean mental health, and not confusing this with mental illness.

Thinking about the broader population, combined with the economic realities of our time, should require us to be able to explain the value of every penny we spend, and it seems likely that current models of mental health care will be unsustainable in the years ahead. Prevention, services for children and a stronger focus on resilience are not just ambitions, they probably represent our only chance of finding a way of providing improved mental health for all. Our aim is to encourage everyone with an interest in mental health to get the best possible return for the effort and resources applied, and a considerable proportion of this book reflects these debates and discussions. Reflected throughout the chapters that follow are themes of well-being, resilience, and extending our awareness of mental health interventions and support into schools and workplaces as well as other everyday settings.

Although placing mental health in a broader health and social context is essential, it should not be done at the expense of those who experience mental ill-health or are using specialist mental health services. We look at the future of mental health services, the results of a major review of current services and likely future trends. We also look at an international example of how to shift from an individual illness model to an approach that focuses on community solutions to community problems. The book also challenges historical thinking on diagnosis and disease, suggesting that there is value in a more rights-based approach that is consistent with contemporary thinking on disability. We also explore the concept of 'parity of esteem', testing whether it is possible or even useful to make comparisons between physical and mental health and, if so, what that would actually look like.

Our approach to this book also marks a significant change in role for mental health service users. Previous editions of this book and its sister publications have provided a platform for promoting effective service user and carer involvement, but in this volume service users and carers are writing on a range of topics that stretches far beyond traditional service user involvement. We write on the language, imagery and interpretations of mental distress, on self-management and peer support, and on leadership.

I have been involved with this series of handbooks for some years now, and I have taken the liberty of tweaking the title. This reflects our desire to encourage people to look forward, and no looking forward would be complete without considering the impact of technology on mental health.

This book has been written during a period of austerity, but I hope that it will also be read in a future period of prosperity and investment. Looking forward is important; it gives us a sense of perspective and should give us something to look forward to. It is also good for our mental health and well-being.

Chapter 1: No time like the present

By Isabella Goldie

'There will be those who say that our recommendations cannot be afforded, particularly in the current economic climate. We say that it is inaction that cannot be afforded, for the human and economic costs are too high. The health and well-being of today's children depend on us having the courage and imagination to rise to the challenge of doing things differently, to put sustainability and well-being before economic growth and bring about a more equal and fair society.'

Sir Michael Marmot, *Fair Society, Healthy Lives* (2010)

Introduction

It is estimated that mental health problems cost the country as much as £105 billion each year, and addressing this is fast becoming one of the biggest public health challenges of our time. We are not only experiencing an unprecedented pressure on public services but the impact can be seen across a whole range of indicators that we use to measure our success as a society, including economic development. The King's Fund report, *Paying the Price* (McCrone *et al*, 2008), outlined the extent of the problem and the concerning projected costs associated with mental health by 2026.

With this in mind, policy makers have turned to the matter of what can be done to minimise the 'failure demand' for acute and long-term services. Across the UK we have been provided with a strategic vision for meeting needs further down the line (Marmot, 2010; Christie Commission, 2011), but what do these directives mean for the way in which we provide and commission services? Many will argue that, at a time when spending across health is contracting, we can't simple turn away from the immediate needs of those in distress to focus on what is effectively a long-term return on our investment. These are debates that we need to have, and balancing our efforts between long-term approaches and immediate needs will be something to grapple with for some time to come.

We can't only look to mental health policy makers to help us to resolve these issues, since much of mental health is made or damaged out in the world where people live their lives. It will take a collaboration of sectors, and working together across areas of interest such as health, education, housing, employment and education will at least enable us to begin this journey towards creating a fairer and mentally healthier society.

Since the start of the 20th century and the growth of public health, we have successfully established the causes of many of the most deadly diseases that were once a mystery, particularly in the case of communicable diseases, and where this has not been possible we are closer to understanding significant contributing/risk factors. This has allowed us – the state and the scientific community – to take action to improve mortality rates.

This is not necessarily the case, however, for mental health, where the issues are more complex and where those living with some mental health conditions experience a mortality gap of between 15–20 years. Conceptually, there remains debate around the etiology of mental health problems and there is a lack of investment in research that would enable us to further discover the factors at play. But there is a growing body of evidence pointing to the determinants of mental health problems and to the adversity that increases risk associated with poor mental health and mental health problems (Felitti & Anda, 1997).

This is surely enough to allow us to act now. Can we justify waiting for the results of further longitudinal studies, which often take decades to provide meaningful results? Given the economic projections and the impact on the life chances of individuals affected, morally this should not even be a consideration.

Prevention

Prevention is a concept widely recognised across public health. As far back as 400BC societies have been concerned with identifying causes, patterns and means of transmission of disease (Hippocrates, 400BC). The science of epidemiology has been a cornerstone of public health and has enabled us to better understand disease risk and to promote evidence-based preventative actions. In public health, preventative actions are commonly applied across three levels:

1. Primary prevention – aiming to stop ill-health occurring by addressing the wider determinants and using long-term approaches that target the majority of the population. Examples include efforts to reduce risky behaviours such as smoking or to improve environmental factors such as poor water sanitation.

2. Secondary prevention – the early identification of health problems and early intervention to minimise progression. A focus for interventions here may be, for example, encouraging a change in eating habits for people who are overweight and at risk of type II diabetes.

3. Tertiary prevention – working with people with established ill-health to prevent further damage to health. Cardiac disease would be one example, where treatment such as drug therapy or surgery may be applied alongside lifestyle advice to prevent further organ damage or to maximise the possibility of recovery.

Prevention has been further categorised to allow for targeting different groups in relation to risk and, when applied to mental health, can be described as:

■ universal prevention: targeting the whole population, groups or settings where there is an opportunity to improve mental health, such as schools or employers

■ selective prevention: targeting individuals or subgroups of the population based on vulnerability and exposure to adversity, such as those living with challenges that are known to be corrosive to mental health (BME communities, people who are homeless, people living with long-term conditions and LGBT people, for example)

■ indicated prevention: targeting people at highest risk of mental health problems, such as employees who are showing signs of workplace stress, children whose parents have a serious mental health problem, children with conduct disorders, looked after young people, socially isolated older people and war veterans.

Unequal lives

Within parts of the UK we are seeing a concerning trend towards increasing health inequalities explained in the main by poor mental health and mental health problems. People with mental health problems experience a range of inequalities:

■ One in ten children aged five to 16 years have a clinically diagnosable mental health problem (depression, anxiety or psychosis) affecting educational attainment, social relationships and overall life chances (Green *et al*, 2005).

■ Each increase in mental health problems is shadowed by poor physical health with a premature mortality gap of 15–20 years for some conditions (Royal College of Psychiatrists & Academy of Medical Royal Colleges, 2009).

■ They are more likely to be socially isolated (Farina *et al*, 1968; Link *et al*, 1989) with more than 50% having poor social contact compared with six per cent of the general population, and they are four times more likely than the general population to be living alone (SAMH, 2006).

■ The rates of employment for people with serious mental health problems can be as low as 20%, compared with a rate of around 50% for disabled people in general and 80% for the population as a whole (Office for National Statistics, 2009).

Mental health impacts negatively on health status overall, and those with health conditions and disabilities are not only found in higher numbers within areas of deprivation but they are also disproportionately affected by mental health problems. This makes mental health our greatest public health issue, yet it continues to receive a fraction of health funding – in some areas, up to three times less than is spent on physical health. Mental health has seen disproportionate cuts compared to acute health services and, given the added austerity-related stresses placed on individuals, including changes to welfare reform and risk of unemployment, many worry that there is a crisis on the horizon (Mental Health Policy Group, 2014).

Reducing the risk of poor health or ameliorating the impact of an existing condition can be complex, often requiring efforts to focus on a range of health behaviours alongside social and environmental factors such as poverty or poor housing. But this is even more complex in relation to mental health where less may be known about the etiology of the condition (see table 1.1).

The bi-lineal relationship between our internal world – our emotions and cognitions – and the context in which we live our lives, means that having a mental health problem can be both a consequence and a cause of socio-economic inequalities. Mental health problems aren't evenly distributed across society and social ills such as being born into poverty make it more likely for problems to develop. The lack of life opportunities and the stress of living a difficult life is challenge enough to our mental health, but this can be compounded by the social stigma attached to having less than others in society and being reliant on social welfare. This stigma can then be internalised, leaving people living with the shame of poverty.

In addition, having a mental health problem can lead to reduced life opportunities that can expose people to further adversity. Our main means of income as individuals comes from employment, however as already mentioned, research reports high rates of unemployment among people with mental health problems, consistently showing levels three to five times higher than those without mental health problems. A number of barriers to employment have been identified, with stigma being significant. This mental health stigma has been shown to shape decisions about recruitment as well as support to sustain employment. People with mental health problems identify employment discrimination as one of their most frequent experiences of stigma. A worrying trend is that mental health problems have become one of the leading causes of absenteeism across the EU, while at the same time evidence shows that employment remains a safeguard against poverty and exclusion.

This level of unemployment inevitably leads to serious financial disadvantage. This means that those with mental health problems face significant challenges securing good quality housing and standards of living, but the disadvantage doesn't stop there, as work is one of the main places where we form social connections and disposable income is vital to our ability to remain socially active.

Promotion vs. prevention

There exists some confusion around the concepts of 'promotion' and 'prevention' in a health context, and they are often considered as one and the same.

Promotion differs from prevention, however, by referring to practices intended to improve health and well-being rather than preventing ill-health and mental health problems. Of course, finding out what works to promote positive health and building on this also diminishes the risk or incidence of ill-health. Promoting exercise as a means of supporting positive physical health is one clear example, since exercise has also been shown to help prevent illness such as heart disease. There is therefore a great deal of overlap between the two, and often prevention strategies operate alongside health promotion.

One issue shared by both health promotion and prevention is that there can be an overreliance on identifying individual health behaviours, and although the way we live our own lives and the responsibility that we take for our own health is important, many are not in a position of great choice. Even in areas where individual responsibility may appear clear, such as obesity, it is not always as straightforward as it first appears. Food options available in supermarkets, spending power to support good decisions, knowledge and understanding of labelling and additives to food, for example, can all play a strong role in determining our choices or lack thereof. This has led some to consider the politics and social construction of health.

It can be usefully argued that where a prevention strategy comes into its own is in focusing on those most vulnerable; interventions can thereby be both tailored to the particular risk factors and measured for impact. This requires an understanding of the determinants of mental health and, as previously discussed, these are complex and often involve a whole range of interrelated influences. Table 1.1 attempts to provide some examples of where the evidence points in relation to factors that can influence mental health. Whether referring to mental health or mental health problems, many of these factors will be the same.

Table 1.1: Some determinants of mental health

Society	Community	Family	Individual
Inequality	Personal safety	Family structure	Lifestyle (diet, exercise, alcohol)
Unemployment levels	Housing and open spaces	Family dynamics & functioning	Attributional style (ie. how events are understood)
Social coherence	Economic status of the community	Genetic makeup	Debt/lack of debt
Education	Isolation & loneliness	Inter-generational contact	Physical health
Health & social care provision	Neighbourliness	Parenting	Relationships

(Adapted from McCulloch & Goldie, 2010)

Over recent years there has been a growing interest in using the mental health and well-being status of our society as a measure of our success, rather than solely depending on GDP. As a result there has been a trend towards promoting well-being in communities through large-scale promotion programmes. Universal approaches have often been adopted in an attempt to shift the population as a whole towards the positive end of the well-being spectrum. There is a body of work in relation to the conceptualisation of well-being that would be beyond the scope of this chapter, however the concept and the adoption of universal approaches has been contested, as has the robustness of the evidence base regarding the effectiveness of well-being approaches.

One such example is the annual report of the Chief Medical Officer (2013), which stated that the investment in relation to well-being 'is running ahead of the evidence'. In this report, Dr Davis accepts that a public mental health approach is the required direction of travel, but states that well-being should be viewed as a subset of such a strategy alongside efforts to prevent mental health problems. The arguments are complex, but working through them will potentially bring important insights.

A settings-based approach

Part of the issue may be that measuring universal health promotion activities is exceedingly challenging. Attributing any change to a single intervention across a whole population would be impossible. People don't live in contained worlds and they can be exposed to many other contaminating influences. Achieving poor results in terms of improved outcomes may not indicate a failure of a programme but could instead result from, for example, an increase in contradictory messages on television or social media. It could even be argued that the health promotion activity had prevented a worsening of health status. Settings such as schools or other, more contained, communities may be the best place to test and evaluate the potential for promoting positive mental health. Indeed, there are systematic reviews that have identified positive changes from school-based skills development programmes.

A notable example of where there has been some success in efforts to improve mental health and well-being in community settings is the GoWell project, which operates across 15 deprived areas in Glasgow, where community investment and regeneration appears to have had an impact on levels of community well-being. A study showed that people in GoWell communities, despite living with high levels of change, ill health, neighbourhood problems and relative poverty, had well-being scores similar to that of the Scottish population as a whole. This was an important finding as it is known that there is a correlation between living in an area of deprivation and experiencing poor mental health and higher rates of mental health problems.

Although this was a cross-sectional study and therefore precludes conclusions about causality, what the study appears to indicate is that there are associations between well-being and feeling that you are living in a neighbourhood that helps you do well in life, where you feel that you have a say and are being heard by those with the power to influence decisions, and where there is a sense of community cohesion.

In schools, mental health promotion initiatives may help to immunise young people against mental health problems in later life by building resilience and, in the interim, create a school culture that is supportive and tolerant of difference (for a more detailed discussion of building resilience and improving mental health and well-being in school settings, see Chapter 4). In general, the role of schools has been shifting towards helping children to build life skills, social and emotional intelligence, and to navigate relationships in ways that will stand them in good stead in adulthood. These are of course admirable aspirations, and although there is more to be discovered about the effectiveness of such approaches it is difficult to imagine that supporting the development of well-rounded children will not pay dividends in terms of mental health in adulthood. Review level evidence does indicate that whole-school multi-modal approaches that work to promote across the whole population but also to prevent poor outcomes for those at risk or showing signs of developing mental health problems can be effective. These should contain three intervention components that work across different levels and take account of risk:

■ systemic – changes to school ethos, teacher education, work with parents, community engagement and co-ordination with other support agencies

■ universal for all pupils – curriculum-based teaching of skills for social problem solving, social awareness and emotional literacy, delivered through active classroom methodologies such as games, simulations and group work

■ targeted – focusing on children with particular issues such as behavioural problems, or other signs of various mental health problems.

Investing in the future

So where to start? As early as possible in the life course appears to be the answer. More than half of mental health problems start before the age of 14, three-quarters of lifetime prevalence arises by the mid-20s and 40% of young people experience at least one mental disorder by age 16. For many, this will lead to negative consequences throughout their lives and can be cumulative.

Intervening to support effective, nurturing parenting is an area where real impact may be possible (for a more detailed discussion of early investment in children's mental health, see Chapter 3). Despite this being a valid and important area for investment, it is a daunting undertaking given the number of new parents emerging each year, and with scarce resources it may pose a significant challenge. Adopting a selective and indicative preventative approach rather than a universal approach is perhaps part of the answer – focusing on risk factors and investing more resources in parents whose children may be at greater risk. This more targeted approach may appear more realistic, although it does have drawbacks, as it may single out and further stigmatise families who perhaps already feel that they are not valued in society.

Taking a universal approach, on the other hand, is not only challenging in relation to resources but may also create health gain over health equity, with parents who already have the personal resources or who feel empowered being among those most receptive or able to access information or interventions. Marmot, in his report *Fair Society Healthy Lives* (2010), poses an interesting potential solution: taking a universally proportionate approach through investing most where it can do the most good.

The World Health Organization (2002) recommends that to improve mental health outcomes, countries should be working to bring together work on mental health promotion and prevention. Importantly, it also acknowledges within its 2013–2020 action plan (WHO, 2013) that addressing vulnerability and exposure to adversity need to be key components of such an approach. It states within objective three that '80% of countries will have at least two functioning national multi-sectoral promotion or prevention programmes by 2020', and that '[these] Programmes preferably should cover both universal, population-level promotion or prevention strategies (e.g. mass media campaigns against discrimination) and those aimed at locally identified vulnerable groups'.

Using the prevention approach illustrated in figure 1.1, it may be possible to take a stepped or tiered approach to invest more heavily in those experiencing the most difficult lives.

Figure 1.1: Embedding a proportionate approach

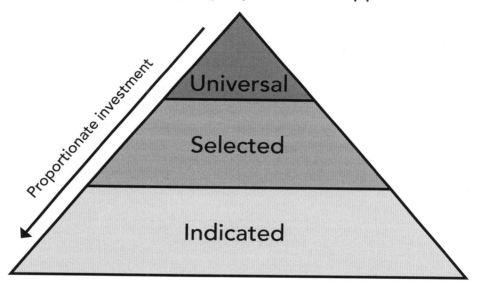

A life-course approach

Opportunities to protect mental health need to begin at conception, thereafter spanning the life course, from cradle to grave. The case to prioritise work with children and their families as an important investment for the future is appealing – public mental health's version of a vaccination programme that seeks to immunise young people against future adverse life events. This is an area where there has not been the needed investment to date, even though we know of the vital importance of mental health in childhood and its effect over the life course. Over many years, a body of evidence has grown that indicates that intervening to improve the mental health of young people is one of the most cost-effective means we have in our public health improvement toolkit (Olds *et al*, 1998). Adverse life events in childhood can impose a massive financial burden on individuals, families and society and are related to a number of poor outcomes. The lack of nurturing, poor attachment or neglect experienced in early years and the resulting trauma can persist and be further compounded by negative outcomes as the child grows up, causing a cumulative effect.

There are children at greater risk, such as those who experience abuse or neglect, or who have poor physical health (Meltzer *et al*, 2003). Home visiting and family-based interventions appear to be effective in promoting improved parenting and outcomes for vulnerable pre-school children (Baxter *et al*, 2012). That being said, we can't turn back the clock. Most people in our society are no longer babies or very young children and it is important to realise that although this is a crucial starting point worthy of special attention, there are also many points on our journey through life when there is an opportunity to take action that may prevent the onset of a mental health problem or reduce the duration, severity or negative outcomes of an episode of illness. Viewing primary prevention in early years as an important area of focus does not mean that primary prevention across the life course or secondary and tertiary prevention are not valid. Adolescence is a time when problems can begin to emerge and provides another pivotal opportunity for early intervention that may improve outcomes in adulthood. Public mental health has seldom viewed work with adolescents as a priority. However, identifying young people who are vulnerable needs to be higher on our agenda. Those with a conduct disorder experience nine times the mortality rates of other young people (Coffrey *et al*, 2003) and 50% of crimes are committed by people who were shown to have a persistent conduct disorder as a child (Moffitt *et al*, 2002).

Thinking back to the determinants of mental health, receiving an education and attaining employment are factors that can be protective. However, entering further education for the first time and beginning or ending working life are transitions that are not always straightforward or rewarding. Factors that support our mental health, such as relationships, employment and community cohesion, can have an adverse effect when people are excluded from these or have negative experiences such as bullying, harassment and abuse. Even though studies have shown that those in retirement are among the happiest in our society, still many experience later life as a lonely time filled with loss. Much suffering can be prevented even at this stage of life. Reducing the impact of dementia on independent living and working to prevent depression in later life are good examples of where lives can be changed for the better (for a more detailed discussion of old age and mental health, see Chapter 9).

Conclusion

Inequality in mental health care means that there exists an unequal distribution of factors that promote and protect positive mental health, and factors that are detrimental to mental health. Despite investment to address social disadvantage, deep inequalities remain in our society with the gap between the richest and poorest increasing (Howell, 2013; Black & O'Sullivan, 2012). Our unequal society and the costs of this to mental health should be a central concern for us all; it leads to an unequal distribution across population groups of mental health problems and illness and in people's ability to recover and lead fulfilling lives.

Until we live in a fairer and more just society, we need to address the chronic stress and fractures that having little power, status and control brings, and we need to work with people to build strong communities and empowering services. To do this effectively will require that we work collaboratively across all areas of policy to influence the factors that serve as determinants of mental health and enable inequalities and disadvantage to grow.

Future investment in mental health needs to take account of the cost of 'failure demand' and find a balance between supporting those in distress now while also working on long-term solutions to create mentally healthier children who will grow into resilient adults. This is nothing new, but still we seem entrenched in the same debates around the efficacy of long-term investment. In answer to this, it may be the time to accept that resources are limited and to invest where we can do the most good. This will mean working to prevent poor outcomes for those most at risk and living the most difficult and often miserable lives: people living in poverty with poor health and long-term conditions, and those that are experiencing discrimination such as racism, ageism and homophobia. For some, all of these issues may be a factor as they often cluster in the same groups and communities.

We need to accept that we can't do everything, but we can ensure that we start early in life with those who will be the parents of the future. In doing so, it is vitally important that we recognise that this is not the only point where we can make a difference, and therefore also invest in prevention across the life course. We have more to learn about what attachment and nurturing could mean beyond early years. We know that adverse life events in childhood can set the stage for poor mental health but there may be more we can do to improve outcomes and prevent further erosion to mental health. At the very least we need to understand what we can do to prevent re-traumatising people who have experienced early adverse life events.

Gathering more evidence of what is most effective in preventing mental health problems, or ameliorating the negative impact they can have on people's lives should be a priority, but this should not lead to inaction now. Research is important, but we also need to be open to a wider approach to learning. In real, messy and complex lives it will not always be either ethical or indeed practical to carry out experimental studies that would provide the best epidemiological evidence. However, testing and evaluating in real-life situations what comprises promising practice, and creating learning cultures across disciplines, needs to be central to any prevention programme.

Universal approaches to primary prevention may be hardest to measure and there may be more to gain from creating tiered approaches within communities or with target groups of people at greater risk where there will be more opportunity to tailor messages and interventions according to need. Marmot (2010) would recommend that we need to invest our prevention efforts in a universally proportionate way and this is worth careful consideration.

Overall, investment in mental health in the UK may be higher than in many countries, but many of our efforts to improve outcomes as a society in relation to economic development, health and equity are underpinned by mental health. Therefore, not only is parity of esteem between health and mental health a valid aspiration, but it is one that needs to move quickly into reality. In the UK we have made a great start on this agenda with the world-leading National Programme for Improving Mental Health and Wellbeing (2003–2008) (NHS Health Scotland, 2008), and, in England, with the appointment of a Mental Health and Wellbeing National Lead to take forward a significant programme of work aimed at promoting public mental health approaches at a number of levels, including gathering data to benchmark progress (www.nepho.org.uk/mho/). In Wales, meanwhile, an emerging public mental health strategy is in development and has invested in reviewing the strongest evidence on most effective and promising practice to underpin this. So, the argument to embed mental health within public health has been made and is being heard; now the challenge will be to mainstream this agenda in the policies and services where we can have most influence on creating a fair, equal and mentally healthy UK.

References

Baxter S, Blank L, Messina J, Fairbrother H, Goyder E & Chilcott J (2012) *Promoting the Social and Emotional Wellbeing of Vulnerable Pre-school Children (0-5 yrs): Systematic review level evidence.* Sheffield: ScHARR.

Black O & O'Sullivan I (Eds) (2012) *Wealth in Great Britain Wave 2: Main results from the wealth and assets survey 2008/2010 (part 3).* London: Office for National Statistics.

Chief Medical Officer (2013) *Public Mental Health Priorities: Investing in the evidence* [online]. Available at: https://www.gov.uk/government/uploads/system/uploads/attachment_data/file/351629/Annual_report_2013_1.pdf (accessed December 2014).

Christie Commission (2011) *Commission on the Future Delivery of Public Services* [online]. Available at: www.gov.scot/about/review/publicservicescommission (accessed December 2014).

Coffey E, Berenbaum H & Kerns JG (2003) The dimensions of emotional intelligence, alexithymia, mood awareness: associations with personality and performance on an emotional stroop task. *Cognition & Emotion* **17** 671–679.

Farina A, Allen JG & Saul BB (1968) The role of the stigmatized in affecting social relationships. *Journal of Personality* **36** (2) 169–182.

Felitti VJ & Anda RF (1997) *Injury Prevention and Control: Division of violence prevention* [online]. Centers for Disease Control and Prevention. Available at: http://www.cdc.gov/ace/index.htm (accessed December 2014).

Green H, McGinnity A, Meltzer H, Ford T & Goodman R (2005) *Mental Health of Children and Young People in Great Britain, 2004*. London: Palgrave.

Hippocrates (400BC) *The Book of Prognostics*.

Howell (2013) *Global Risks 2013 Eighth Edition: An initiative of the risk response network*. Switzerland: World Economic Forum.

Kings Fund (2008) *Paying the Price* [online]. Available at: http://www.kingsfund.org.uk/publications/paying-price (accessed March 2015).

Link BG, Cullen FT, Struening EL, Shrout PE & Dohrenwend BP (1989) A modified labeling theory approach to mental disorders and empirical assessment. *American Sociological Review* **54** 400–423.

Marmot M (2010) *Fair Society, Healthy Lives: Strategic review of health inequalities in England post 2010* [online]. Available at: www.marmotreview.org (accessed December 2014).

McCrone P, Dhanasiri S, Patel A, Knapp M & Lawton-Smith S (2008) *Paying the Price: The cost of mental health care in England to 2026*. London: King's Fund.

McCulloch A & Goldie I (2010) Introduction. In: I Goldie (Ed) *Public Mental Health Today: A handbook* (2010). Brighton: Pavilion Publishing.

Meltzer M, Gatward R, Corbin T, Goodman R & Ford T (2003) *The Mental Health of Young People Looked After by Local Authorities in England*. London: TSO.

Mental Health Policy Group (2014) *A Manifesto for Better Mental Health* [online]. Available at: http://www.mentalhealth.org.uk/content/assets/PDF/publications/manifesto-better-mental-health-manifesto.pdf (accessed December 2014).

Moffitt TE, Caspi A, Harrington H, Milne BJ (2002) Males on the life-course-persistent and adolescence-limited antisocial pathways: follow-up at age 26 years. *Development and Psychopathology* **14** (1) 179–207.

NHS Health Scotland (2008) *A Review of Scotland's National Programme for Improving Mental Health and Wellbeing* [online]. Available at: http://www.healthscotland.com/uploads/documents/6017-MENTAL%20HEALTH.pdf (accessed December 2014).

Office for National Statistics (2009) *Labour Market Statistics* [online]. Available at: http://www.ons.gov.uk/ons/rel/lms/labour-market-statistics/index.html (accessed December 2014).

Olds D, Henderson CR Jr, Cole R, Eckenrode J, Kitzman H, Luckey D, Pettitt L, Sidora K, Morris P & Powers J (1998) Long-term effects of nurse home visitation on children's criminal and antisocial behavior: 15-year follow-up of a randomized controlled trial. *Journal of the American Medical Association* **280** (14) 1238–1244.

Royal College of Psychiatrists & Academy of Medical Royal Colleges (2009) *No Health Without Mental Health: The ALERT summary report.* London: Academy of Medical Royal Colleges.

SAMH (2006) *What's it Worth?* Glasgow: Scottish Association for Mental Health.

World Health Organization (2002) *Prevention and Promotion in Mental Health.* Geneva: WHO.

World Health Organization (2013) *Mental Health Action Plan 2013–2020* [online]. Geneva: WHO. Available at: http://www.who.int/mental_health/publications/action_plan/en/ (accessed March 2015).

Chapter 2: Mental well-being: concepts and controversies in mental health policy and practice

By Sarah Stewart-Brown

Introduction

The term 'mental well-being' has been appearing in both mental and public health policy in the UK for the last decade (eg. Department of Health, 2004; 2010; HM Government, 2011; UK Government Office for Science, 2008). Before that, positive aspects of mental health were variously referred to as 'positive mental health', 'psychological well-being' or 'emotional resilience' (eg. Department of Health, 1999) and were addressed primarily in the writings of health promotion specialists. Although some have used the term 'wellness' as the antithesis of illness, well-being seems to be the word that has found favour in the world of mental health policy and practice, in keeping with the World Health Organization's seminal pronouncement over half a century ago that 'health is a state of mental, physical and social well-being' (World Health Organization, 1948).

On the face of it, the term 'well-being' seems pretty innocuous. Most of us know about feeling well, just as we know about feeling ill. And most of us would recognise that we don't feel well when troubled by anxiety, depression or other negative emotional states any more than we do when we are troubled by physical ailments. But for an innocuous word, well-being seems to have the power to generate a great deal of controversy, as illustrated most recently in the report of the Chief Medical Officer for England (Chief Medical Officer, 2014) in which she has advised strongly against commissioning services to promote mental well-being on the grounds that the concept was not sufficiently well defined and that the evidence base to support interventions was poor.

This chapter aims to address some of those controversies and to outline my views on the nature of mental well-being. These views have been developing over the last 20 years, partly as a result of working as an academic in the field of public mental health, partly working as a public health practitioner, and partly in addressing my own mental health and well-being and its origins in a family in which serious mental illness is common. I have learnt a great deal from the writings of academic colleagues in psychology, social science, psychiatry and child health, and from teachers of both Eastern and Western approaches to personal and spiritual development. I have also learnt from observation of myself and my family as I have experimented with these different approaches. So, while I don't claim any of my ideas as original, I also don't claim that they follow the thinking of any one individual or approach alone.

A model of mental health

One thing that is agreed about mental well-being is that it represents more than simply the absence of mental illness. Figure 2.1 shows the way I see mental well-being fitting into the mental health picture. It shows mental health as the general term covering a whole spectrum from positive to negative, while mental illness covers the negative aspects of mental health and mental well-being covers the positive. These two aspects are set against a backdrop of the middle ground, which includes most of the population. It also depicts both mental illness and mental well-being as porous states into which people can come and go.

For mental illness, this is in line with observation. Somewhere between a quarter and a half of us experience mental illness of clinical severity during our lifetimes, but only around 10% of adults have a mental illness of this severity at any one point in time and fewer still are in the care of psychiatrists (Chief Medical Officer, 2014). This means that mental illness severe enough to warrant a psychiatric diagnosis must be able to come and go. In psychiatric services, especially for those with severe mental illnesses like bipolar disorders and schizophrenia, a diagnosis of mental illness tends to be regarded as a permanent label and so seems to conflict with the basis of figure 2.1. While the latter may reflect the experience of psychiatrists, which suggests that it is unusual to recover from severe mental illness sufficiently to lead a normal life, it is possible and it does happen. On the other hand, it is not unusual to recover completely from one of the common mental disorders like anxiety and depression.

Figure 2.1: A model of mental health

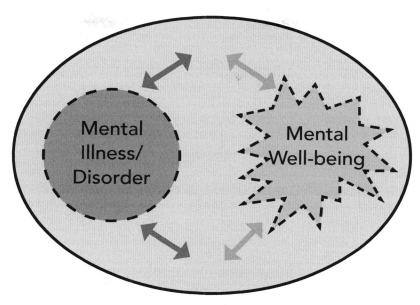

In figure 2.1, mental well-being is depicted similarly to mental illness as a state from which people come and go, rather than a permanent one. Everyone, including those who have at some stage of their lives been unwell enough to be given psychiatric diagnoses, could therefore achieve this state for some of their lives, but few are likely to live permanently like this.

What is mental well-being?

Well-being is a state that philosophers have pondered on and written about more or less since writing began. Sometimes couched in terms of 'routes to happiness', these writings have offered insights and advice from the study of the literature, observation of others and personal reflection. We tend to think of the ancient Greeks and of the early philosophers like Aristotle, from whom we have the term eudaimonic well-being, and Epicurus, from whom we have the term hedonic well-being, as the main contributors.

Hedonic approaches to mental well-being recommend maximising pleasure and minimising pain and are usually measured by questions about happiness or satisfaction with life. Eudaimonic approaches advise living authentically in accordance with one's inherent nature, and behaving virtuously, emphasising things like justice, kindness, courage and honesty.

The East has also provided its share of philosophers. Some, like those who contributed to the Vedas and Upanishads, and the Buddha, come from a more spiritual perspective while others, such as Confucius, from a secular one. Meditation is an important component of many of these Eastern spiritual traditions.

Recently, contributions have come from psychologists who have defined concepts like psychological well-being (Ryff & Keyes, 1995). The latter focuses on the development of high level skills and capacities like self-acceptance, autonomy, agency, good relationships with others and personal development, which reflect the eudaimonic approaches of the ancient Greeks. Positive psychologists have also contributed the concepts of flourishing (Keyes, 2002), flow (Czikszentmihalyi, 1991), coherence (Antonovsky, 1987) authentic happiness (Seligman, 2002) and emotional intelligence (Goleman, 1995). The latter is a key relationship skill and so contributes to positive relationships with others, an important component of psychological well-being and flourishing.

Authentic happiness has a flavour of hedonic approaches in recommending that the route to happiness is to identify the things that give deep satisfaction and do more of them. Social and political scientists have also taken an interest in well-being from the hedonic perspective, often focusing on the societal rather than individual causes. Their research looks at the social, political and fiscal contributions to mental well-being and uses measures of happiness and life satisfaction.

Feeling good and functioning well

Most of those working in the field of mental well-being are now coming to agree that it involves both feeling good (hedonic perspective) and functioning well (eudaimonic perspective) (Henderson & Knight, 2012). Reflection on these two apparently opposing perspectives shows that they are linked in several different ways. The skills and capacities of eudaimonia and psychological well-being, for example, enhance happiness and life satisfaction because it is satisfying to live authentically in accordance with one's nature and because personal happiness is dependent on the happiness of other people. The capacity for personal development and for making sense of problems and setbacks, like the experience of mental illness (other eudaimonic skills), also enables people to be happier more of the time.

And it is of course much easier to develop new eudaimonic skills, capacities and insights when one is enjoying life (hedonic well-being) rather than when living with a high level of pain and distress. Knowing yourself and your needs and ensuring that you make time for the things that give you pleasure therefore enable eudaimonic well-being. A definition of mental well-being that encompasses both feeling good and functioning well counter-balances the criteria for diagnosing mental illness, which almost invariably involves aspects of feeling bad and functioning poorly.

Extending the definition

The teachings of Eastern philosophers and spiritual leaders seem to me to take the understanding of mental well-being a step further. While the term 'mental well-being' is not often used in translations of their work, it is implicitly addressed and offers an understanding of the state which I understand as one in which people:

- know themselves and their needs well
- recognise themselves in others and make relationships from a compassionate, respectful perspective that takes the needs of self and others into account
- take responsibility for themselves and their actions
- create and maintain clear boundaries in human relationships
- work because it is meaningful and valuable, not because it enhances wealth, status or power over others
- enjoy rest as well as activity.

This view extends the definition of mental well-being beyond that in the Western literature and may or may not accord with those of other experts – it needs discussing, debating and testing. In contrast to the Chief Medical Officer (2014), I do not see the fact that we have yet to arrive at a clear, universally agreed and succinct definition of mental well-being as a problem. I have found, and expect others have as well, that as I have reflected on my own well-being and developed more well-being skills and capacities, my definition of well-being has become more subtle and sophisticated.

Some of the things that I have understood will be recognised as true by those who are also engaging at this level, but may not be so clear to those who have given well-being little thought. The Eskimos are said to have recognised and given names to many different qualities of snow. This has happened because snow is something to which they have paid a lot of attention. Understanding of mental well-being, and the sophistication and subtlety of the language we use to describe its various attributes and components, is bound to grow and develop as it starts to occupy a greater space in our lives and as we explore this concept both for ourselves and for society as a whole. As this happens, definitions and descriptions will become more precise.

There is good reason to suppose that there are as many ways in which mental health can be compromised as there are ways in which physical health can be compromised and thus as many ways in which we can be mentally well. The Chief Medical Officer argues that we should not develop policies and programmes before we entirely understand the end point or goal, but this argument is not one that has been adopted in other areas of public health practice. We started programmes to reduce elevated blood pressure and cholesterol levels before we knew the optimum level for either. We are very clear that increasing the level of physical activity individuals undertake would benefit the health of the population even though we do not yet know what sort of exercise, how much and how frequently is appropriate for optimising health for people of different ages and constitutions.

One spectrum or more

One important and topical discussion focuses on whether mental illness and mental well-being are at opposite ends of one spectrum. The dual continuum model (Keyes, 2005) is based on studies that show that people with a diagnosis of mental illness can report high levels of mental well-being and some of those with poor mental well-being do not have a diagnosed psychiatric illness.

Figure 2.2: The dual continuum model

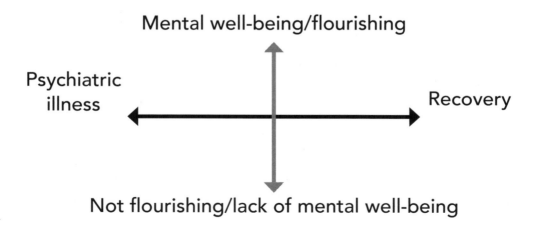

(Keyes, 2005)

This model has found favour with psychiatrists whose services focus on diagnosing psychiatric disorder and treating the symptoms that prevent patients from engaging in society in a meaningful way. These treatments are often pharmacological. If they involve talking therapies, these often focus on problems and deficits and what can be done to overcome them. They rarely focus on assets or strengths and are designed to reduce mental illness not to enhance well-being. At the same time, knowledge of well-being and well-being interventions is growing.

The practice of mindfulness, which is directly derived from Eastern spiritual traditions and implicitly addresses well-being, is growing in some psychiatric services. The use of acupuncture in drug misuse services and in the community for depression and anxiety is also based on well-being models. But well-being approaches remain uncommon and, some would argue, in services that are under-resourced, they are not practical. So it makes sense to many mental illness service providers to see well-being as something that should be addressed outside mental health services.

The dual continuum model has also found favour with users of psychiatric services who are often told that their diagnosis is lifelong and thus a life sentence. If mental illness is presented as at the opposite end of a single continuum from mental well-being, then a diagnosis of, for example, bipolar disorder, would seem to exclude users from the experience of well-being, unless of course the relapsing and remitting nature of mental illness is taken into account.

A recent study of a web-based cognitive behaviour therapy programme (Powell *et al*, 2013) collected data from participants using both the CES-D (Radloff, 1977), a clinically validated measure of depression, and WEMWBS – the Warwick-Edinburgh Mental Well-being Scale (Tennant *et al*, 2007). The correlation between scores on these two measures was very high, apparently contradicting the dual continuum model (see figure 2.3).

More studies are needed to investigate the dual continuum model. From my perspective it is entirely possible that people who have been diagnosed at some stage in their life with a psychiatric disorder will, at other stages, experience mental well-being. Indeed, the experience of mental illness can set people on a course of personal development and give them a deeper and more robust perspective on mental well-being than is easily available to those who have not faced the challenge of mental illness. What I find hard to accept is that people who are currently mentally unwell – experiencing deep depression, anxiety or paranoid delusions, for example – would at that moment say they are experiencing mental well-being.

Figure 2.3: Close correlation between scores of mental well-being and depression

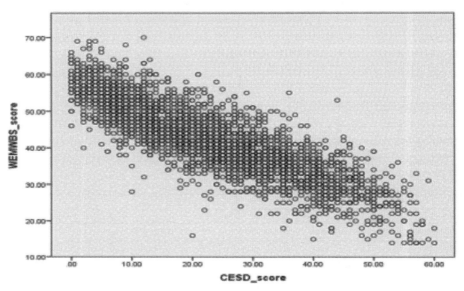

WEMWBS vs CES-D

Pearson Correlation Coefficient 0.842

(Bianca, 2012)

Well-being is holistic

Mental well-being is just one component of a wider concept that encompasses physical well-being and, in some schema, social and/or spiritual well-being. This is sometimes just called 'well-being', but as in the WHO definition of 1948, may also be called 'health'. Well-being seems to me to be a better term because health is often used colloquially and in the names of services to cover illness and disease, rather than being reserved for the positive end of the spectrum.

The connection between mental and physical health (using the terms to cover the spectra from positive to negative) is observable with a little personal reflection and observation of others. People who develop a physical illness often find that this affects them emotionally and people who experience stress or anxiety will often note physical manifestations like susceptibility to infections or musculoskeletal pain. For reasons that are sometimes difficult to understand, for most of the 20th century the medical profession has behaved as though there is no connection between mental and physical health, espousing what has been called the Cartesian divide.

This idea is based on the writings of Descartes, which have been interpreted as saying that the mind and body work independently. In fact, every emotion has a physiological correlate and a neuromuscular one, too. We can tell a lot about how people are feeling in the moment, and as a habitual position, from their body posture. We can also do this with animals and very young children. The facial and bodily expressions of fear, sadness and shame are instantly interpretable across all human races because they are manifested not just as feelings but as neuromuscular patterns (Ekman & Keltner, 1997). Neuromuscular tension is often painful and, if prolonged or common, leads to wear and tear on bones and joints, and eventually to dysfunction and disease. The same process happens in the digestive, immune and respiratory systems, so negative emotions eventually lead to physical illness.

Many negative emotions have an impact on physical health by activating the sympathetic nervous system, which is responsible for the 'flight or fight' response, and switches off digestive, immune and repair processes, raising blood pressure and heart rate. Cortisol, one of the hormones released under stress, has been used for years as an effective anti-inflammatory drug, but if taken over long periods of time is toxic to almost all of the body's physiological processes. This is why it is not surprising that long-term studies show that people with higher levels of mental well-being tend to live longer than those with lower levels (Chida & Steptoe, 2008).

At the other end of the spectrum, it is possible to feel a high degree of mental well-being while also having a physical disability, but it would be unusual to find someone who reports mental well-being while they are in pain or unwell physically, because mental well-being is experienced in the body as well as the mind.

The physical health of those with severe mental illness has been much in the news recently because of the shocking studies showing that life expectancy of people diagnosed with schizophrenia is 12–15 years less than those without (Chief Medical Officer, 2014). Part of this is due to the effects of medication and part to unhealthy lifestyles, like smoking, sedentary behaviour and unhealthy eating, but part of it cannot be attributed to any of these things. Unhealthy lifestyles are, for some people, a response to the stressful business of living with mental illness. Medication for symptoms of mental illness does not address the physiological effects of mental illness on the body, whereas well-being interventions have a reasonable chance of doing so.

Social determinants of mental well-being

The relationship between mental illness and social factors like income, education and employment has been much studied by social scientists. These well-known and marked 'social inequalities' affect physical as well as mental illness and have been the subject of concern to those working in public health for many years

Figure 2.4: Income and mental illness prevalence

Adults in the poorest fifth are much more likely to be at risk of developing a mental illness than those on average incomes.

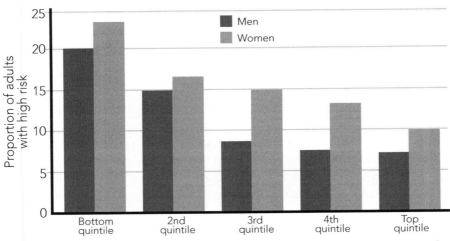

DH Health Survey for England (from www.poverty.org.uk), the data is the average for 2006 and 2008 for England

(From *Monitoring Poverty and Social Exclusion* by Anushree Parekh, Tom MacInnes and Peter Kenway, published in 2010 by the Joseph Rowntree Foundation. Reproduced by permission of the Joseph Rowntree Foundation.)

As mental well-being has begun to capture the interest of researchers, studies are beginning to emerge that aim to look at the social correlates of mental well-being as well as mental illness. Figures 2.5 and 2.6 depict the increased probability of experiencing low mental well-being, which is closely correlated with mental illness (see Figure 2.3), and high mental well-being compared to people whose mental well-being is mid-range. In Figures 2.5 and 2.6, on the left are the probabilities of low mental well-being and on right of high mental well-being.

Figure 2.5 shows these probabilities for educational achievement with the classic distribution on the left: the less education someone has, the greater the probability of them suffering from mental illness. The distribution for high mental well-being is on the right, showing that more education does not increase the probability of mental well-being.

Figure 2.5: Distribution of low and high mental well-being by education

(Adjusted for age, sex, income, employment status, marital status, ethnicity, religion)

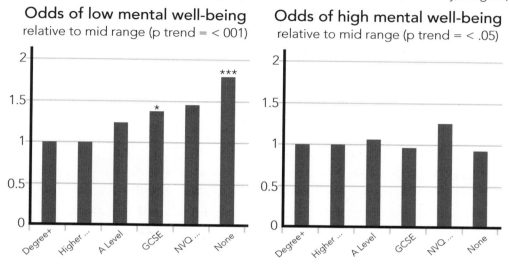

Reference category Degree Level Education

(Stewart-Brown *et al*, 2015)

Figure 2.6 shows these patterns for employment status. The unemployed and those seeking work have a higher probability of poor mental well-being, but the probability of high mental well-being does not differ by employment categories apart from the retired group whose chances of experiencing mental well-being are increased.

Although at first sight it may seem counterintuitive that these contradictory patterns can both be true, it may be that social inequalities in mental illness are a marker of an unhealthy society rather than a key determinant. We know that mental health problems in childhood are a potent cause of educational failure because the symptoms of mental illness – anxiety and depression – affect the capacity to understand new ideas and store information in memory.

We also know that most mental illness has its origins in childhood. Any causal relationship is therefore likely to travel more in the direction of mental illness causing educational failure than the other way round. While those with high mental well-being may have an easier time with educational achievement, they are also good at finding a way of living that accords with their needs, which may not require higher educational qualifications.

Figure 2.6: Distribution of low and high mental well-being by employment status

(Adjusted for age, sex, income, employment status, marital status, ethnicity, religion)

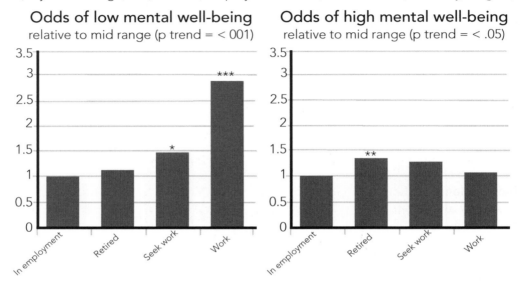

Reference category in employment

(Stewart-Brown *et al*, 2015)

With regard to employment, there are those who choose to stay at home and care for others (classified as unemployed) who are very fulfilled by that role, as well as those who find it extremely stressful. People experiencing mental illness find it hard to maintain productivity in stressful and demanding jobs and so are at risk of unemployment.

This may not be how the world should be. A strong case can be made on both humanitarian and economic grounds for employment policies that respect the needs and strengths of those who experience mental illness. The statistics, however, suggest that the world is not how it should be. While the loss of a job is very stressful and may tip some into a state of mental illness, it can also be an opportunity to change direction, undertake personal development and find work that is more rewarding. So the relationship between employment and mental health is a complicated one and it is perhaps not surprising that mental illness shows different patterns of association from mental well-being.

Status discrimination and stigma

The social determinants of illness have been much studied. Some of this research has been brought together by Richard Wilkinson who has written about the physiological effects of social inequality and being discriminated against or regarded as socially inferior (Wilkinson & Pickett, 2009). He has argued very strongly that a more equal society is key to improving public health, but it is possible that the pursuit of mental well-being presents solutions to both problems. People with high mental well-being have a strong and realistic sense of themselves and their needs. They are less susceptible to the negative views of others, both mentally and physically, and the experience of discrimination or bullying thus becomes unpleasant rather than damaging to health.

As mental well-being develops, people move from being very dependent on the views of others in forming and maintaining their self-image to being independent of others, not so that they take no notice of others' views, but so that they are able to disregard those that do not ring true. People with mental well-being are also more respectful of others and their needs and sensitivities, so they do not themselves discriminate or bully. Structural changes in society, new laws and policies, can reduce the opportunities for people to act in negative ways towards one another, but they cannot eliminate them, especially in the home where this can be most damaging. They cannot eliminate them because the change required to stop discriminating or bullying involves personal development on the part of those who are behaving in this way. And personal development is not something that it is easy to do under coercion. The starting point for personal development is often acceptance of the way things are. So policies and programmes that aim to enhance everyone's mental well-being are also important, as they increase the proportion of the population to whom it is self-evident that behaving negatively towards others is counterproductive to their own as well as others' well-being.

Well-being in the mentally ill

Where does that leave people who use mental health services? Potentially, the mental well-being agenda is a very empowering one for this group as well as for those who experience mental illness but do not receive services. It is empowering because it leaves people less dependent on others and more in the driving seat of their own destiny. But there is a balance to be struck. Anyone who is very unwell, either physically or mentally, needs protecting and supporting because illness is a dependent, vulnerable state. High-quality mental health services are fundamental when they are needed.

However, it is possible to take care of and treat people who are seriously ill until they are well enough to support themselves, but it is not possible for services to give people mental well-being. This is an agenda in which we all need to engage for ourselves. It is possible and valuable to provide supportive services and environments but it is not possible to create the state of mental well-being in another, because the capacity to meet our own needs and to live independently is part of mental well-being. Psychiatric services could provide people who are recovering from bouts of mental illness with support for personal development; they can certainly signpost and could provide more of the sort of things that are known to help, like green spaces, physical activity, creative endeavour, music, relationship skills and mindfulness skills.

For people experiencing mental illness, getting the right balance between supporting dependency and generating independence is the key to enhancing the capacity of the mental well-being agenda in the mentally ill. At present, NHS services in the UK prioritise supporting dependency. If services are to enhance health as well as treat illness they need to move towards supporting the capacity for personal development, first and foremost among which is the development of skills and capacities for mental well-being. Also at present, NHS services do not make the contribution to public health that they need to if the NHS is to survive and flourish as a publicly funded service, because they focus on illness and disease to the exclusion of well-being.

Why such controversy?

Users and carers of mental health services have campaigned for some years for more well-being, less treatment-oriented mental health services, and it is valuable to end this chapter by reflecting on the reasons why this apparently simple agenda seems so difficult to implement. One of the reasons is the availability of resources. Mental health services have been the Cinderella of the NHS, receiving a very low proportion of the overall budget relative to need. When resources are scarce it is more difficult to bring about change, partly because staff are too busy to think about new ideas and approaches and partly because there are no resources to fund experimentation.

Another important reason is that focusing on the positive is unfamiliar to doctors and nurses. Their training is orientated towards disease and ways to look after people who are sick. Supporting and empowering people to take charge of their own lives and to seek well-being is a different skill, and not one that is well taught in medical or nursing schools. Some health professionals learn it for themselves, but if the health service is to enable people to move to a higher level of health rather than just palliating and supporting people who are ill, this is a skill all health professionals need to develop.

Since well-being is holistic, this skill development needs to happen in generic and physical health services too. The starting point for such a shift is to rebalance the focus of medicine away from the disease perspective into a position where both illness and weakness are equally regarded and resourced with well-being and strengths.

References

Antonovsky A (1987) *Unraveling the Mystery of Health: How people manage stress and stay well*. San Fransisco: The Jossey-Bass Social and Behavioral Science Series.

Bianca D (2012) *Performance of the Warwick-Edinburgh Mental Well-Being Scale (WEMWBS) as a Screening Tool for Depression in UK and Italy* [online]. Available at: http://www2.warwick.ac.uk/fac/med/research/platform/wemwbs/development/papers/donatella_bianco-thesis.pdf (accessed December 2014).

Chida Y & Steptoe A (2008) Positive psychological well-being and mortality: a quantitative review of prospective observational studies. *Psychosomatic Medicine* **70** (7) 741– 56.

Chief Medical Officer (England) (2014) *Annual Report of the Chief Medical Officer 2013. Public Mental Health Priorities: Investing in the evidence* [online]. Available at: https://www.gov.uk/government/uploads/system/uploads/attachment_data/file/351629/Annual_report_2013_1.pdf (accessed December 2014).

Czikszentmihalyi M (1991) *Flow: The psychology of optimal experience*. New York: Harper Perennial.

Department of Health (UK) (1999) *Modern Standards and Service Models: A national service framework for mental health* [online]. Available at: https://www.gov.uk/government/uploads/system/uploads/attachment_data/file/198051/National_Service_Framework_for_Mental_Health.pdf (accessed December 2014).

Department of Health (UK) (2004) *Choosing Health: Making healthy choices easier* [online]. Available at: http://webarchive.nationalarchives.gov.uk/+/dh.gov.uk/en/publicationsandstatistics/publications/publicationspolicyandguidance/dh_4094550 (accessed December 2014).

Department of Health (England) (2010) *Healthy Lives, Healthy People: Our strategy for public health in England* [online]. Available at: https://www.gov.uk/government/uploads/system/uploads/attachment_data/file/216096/dh_127424.pdf (accessed December 2014).

Ekman P & Keltner D (1997) Universal facial expressions of emotion: an old controversy and new findings. In: U Segerstrale and P Molnar (Eds) *Non-verbal Communication: Where nature meets culture*. New Jersey: Lawrence Erlbaum Associates.

Goleman D (1995) *Emotional Intelligence*. New York: Bantam Books.

Henderson LW & Knight T (2012) Integrating the hedonic and eudaimonic perspectives to more comprehensively understand well-being and pathways to well-being. *International Journal of Well-being 2* (3) 196–221.

HM Government (2011) *No Health Without Mental Health: A cross-government mental health outcomes strategy for people of all ages* [online]. Available at: https://www.gov.uk/government/uploads/system/uploads/attachment_data/file/213761/dh_124058.pdf (accessed December 2014).

Keyes CLM (2002) The mental health continuum: from languishing to flourishing in life. *Journal of Health and Social Research* **43** (2) 207–222.

Keyes CLM (2005) Mental illness and/or mental health? Investigating axioms of the complete state model of health. *Journal of Consulting and Clinical Psychology* **73** (3) 539–548.

Parekh A, MacInnes T & Kenway P (2010) *Monitoring Poverty and Social Exclusion* [online]. York: Joseph Rowntree Foundation. Available at: http://www.poverty.org.uk/reports/mpse%202010.pdf (accessed December 2014).

Powell J, Hamborg T, Stallard N, Burls A, McSorley J, Bennett K, Griffiths KM & Christensen C (2013) Effectiveness of a web-based cognitive-behavioral tool to improve mental well-being in the general population: randomized controlled trial. *Journal of Medical Internet Research* **5** (1): e2.

Radloff LS (1977) The CES-D Scale. *Applied Psychological Measurement* **1** (3) 385–401.

Ryff C & Keyes C (1995) The structure of psychological well-being revisited. *Journal of Personality and Social Psychology* **69** (4) 719–727.

Seligman MEP (2002) *Authentic Happiness: Using the new positive psychology to realise your potential for lasting fulfilment*. New York: The Free Press.

Stewart-Brown S, Chandimali Samaraweera P, Taggart F & Stranges S (2015) Socio-economic gradients and mental health: implications for public health. *British Journal of Psychiatry* **206**.

Tennant R, Hiller L, Fishwick R, Platt S, Joseph S, Weich S, Parkinson J, Secker J & Stewart-Brown S (2007) The Warwick-Edinburgh Mental Well-Being Scale (WEMWBS): development and UK validation. *Health and Quality of Life Outcomes* **5** (63) doi:10.1186/1477-7525-5-63.

UK Government Office for Science (2008) *Mental Capital and Well-being: Making the most of ourselves in the 21st century* [online]. Available at: https://www.gov.uk/government/uploads/system/uploads/attachment_data/file/292453/mental-capital-well-being-summary.pdf (accessed December 2014).

Wilkinson R & Pickett K (2009) *The Spirit Level: Why equality is better for everyone*. London. Penguin Books.

World Health Organization (1948) Preamble to the Constitution of the World Health Organization as adopted by the International Health Conference, New York, 19–22 June, 1946; signed on 22 July 1946 by the representatives of 61 States (Official Records of the World Health Organization, no. 2, p. 100) and entered into force on 7 April 1948.

Chapter 3: Early investment in children's mental health

By Barbara McIntosh

The framework for a child's future mental health is often set in the first three years of life. Neglectful parenting and/or adverse life events in the early years can profoundly affect long-term development. This chapter uses the growing evidence base to argue for an investment in prevention. It describes examples of successful early interventions and looks at the long-term gains for children, their families and society as a whole when this shift is achieved.

The early years: setting the framework for good mental health

'The earliest years in a child's life influence future health, mental health and life chances. There is overwhelming evidence that the foundations are laid in the first years of life which if weak can have a permanent and detrimental impact on children's longer term development. A child's future choices, attainment, well-being, happiness, and resilience are all profoundly affected by the quality of the guidance, love and care they receive during these first years.'

(Tickell, 2011)

The rapidly growing brain of an infant is responsive to positive interactions and good relationships, which can help develop the brain's physical structure (neuroplasticity) and drive its growth. This rapid growth, both physically and mentally, when combined with nurturing carers, provides the most important opportunity in a person's life for the development of positive mental health and healthy brain development (Allen, 2011). Not only does a supportive and nurturing relationship with parents or carers promote brain development, but also the growth of resilience, the regulation of emotions and empathy. It also has a vital impact on future relationships and learning.

This parent-child relationship is a process of mutual adaptation. Patterns of interactions formed during the early stages of life create a framework for social engagement skills, playing a key role in social and emotional functioning throughout life (Niedenthal *et al*, 2002; Fraley *et al*, 2006; Mikulincer & Shaver, 2006). Interaction with caregivers during the first three years of life actively contributes to shaping psychobiological regulatory processes and the development of the brain's neural pathways, which are most adaptable at this stage but which become more difficult to 'rewire' as the child grows up. Attachment between parent and child is therefore the biological and emotional process that drives behavioural, emotional and social development in every child.

For intervention, the earliest years almost certainly include the gestational period. Experiencing stress in pregnancy can cause high levels of cortisol in a woman's body, which in turn has a toxic effect on the foetal brain (Dana Corporation, 2012) and can have long-lasting effects on the developing brain of the baby. Supporting at-risk mothers during pregnancy and targeting families who have had problems in the past can therefore make a positive difference to a child's long-term life chances.

Deserving better

Chapter 10 of the Chief Medical Officer's annual report *Our Children Deserve Better: Prevention Pays* reviews much of the evidence on prevention and early intervention (Department of Health, 2013; Murphy & Fonagy, 2012).

The report found that one in 10 children and young people under the age of 16 had a diagnosable mental health disorder. Among five to 10 year olds, 10% of boys and five per cent of girls had a mental health problem, while among the 11 to 16 year olds the prevalence was 13% for boys and 10% for girls. Prevention programmes and early support to infants and parents are seen as key factors in decreasing the incidence of mental health problems for future generations of UK children.

There are strong links between mental health problems in children and young people at social disadvantage, with children and young people in the poorest households three times more likely to have a mental health problem than those growing up in better-off homes. The British child and adolescent mental health surveys in 1999 and 2004 (ONS, 1999; Green *et al*, 2005) found that the prevalence of mental disorder was higher in children and young people where there was parental unemployment, a reconstituted family, low levels of parental education or low income. Children who have experienced abuse, those who have been in care and those who have foetal alcohol syndrome or have been exposed to parents with substance abuse problems are all at greater risk of developing mental health problems. Parental mental illness is also associated with increased rates of mental health problems in children and young people, with an estimated one-third to two-thirds of children and young people whose parents have a mental health problem experiencing difficulties themselves.

And just as good attachment and positive relationships can have life-long effects, so too can the problems that these negative circumstances often create. Children with conduct disorders, for example, are twice as likely to leave school without any qualifications, three times more likely to become a teenage parent, four times more likely to become dependent on drugs, eight times more likely to be on the child protection register and 20 times more likely to end up in prison (Grauberg, 2014). Recent neurobiological research has also shown that depression in young children left untreated creates a more resistant form of depression later on in a child's life – another argument for early intervention (Balbernie & Barrows, 2004).

Thus, the consequences of an infant experiencing poor parenting, aggressive treatment or neglect can be life-long. Outcomes can include depression, anxiety, behavioural, emotional and relationship problems, poor achievement at school, and entry into the criminal justice system. Universal support for all mothers/ families starting in pregnancy, and targeted support to vulnerable mothers, can help prevent these problems.

Failing to do so is expensive, not only for the child's life but financially for society. Mental health problems in children and young people are associated with excess costs estimated as being between £11,030 and £59,130 annually per child. These costs fall to a variety of agencies (eg. education, social services and youth justice) and also include the direct costs to the child's family.

Attachment

When there are difficulties with the parent-infant relationship or psychological issues from the parent's own past or present relationships, the family struggle often results in children who are not securely attached. Attachment theory helps us to understand how disturbed attachment passes from one generation to the next and hinders the development of infants and young children. This group frequently goes on to develop significant disturbances in later childhood and early adulthood, as suggested by longitudinal studies (Lyons-Ruth, 2008). The impact of the parent-child relationship therefore stretches well beyond the early years, influencing children's social and emotional well-being and life chances as adults.

We know that 'maternal sensitivity' (Ainsworth *et al*, 1971) and 'mind-mindedness' (Meins *et al*, 2013) are key in the development of infants' and young children's secure attachment, which in turn is associated with a better socio-emotional adjustment and higher resilience throughout childhood and adolescence. These factors are related to the ability of parent figures to recognise the infant as a unique individual, to effectively read his/her mental state and to respond in a prompt, appropriate and consistent manner.

Effective interventions

There is a growing body of evidence that demonstrates how early, targeted and strength-based interventions focusing on relationships between infants and their caregivers can bring about positive changes in the emotional environment of vulnerable children. Not only is it cost effective, but intervening early when a child first shows signs of emotional or mental health problems is far more beneficial than trying to treat what has developed into a serious disorder later in life (NICE, 2012; Allen, 2011).

Much of this evidence is summarised in Chapter 10 of the Chief Medical Officer's annual report (Department of Health, 2013; Murphy & Fonagy, 2012). The authors cite The Evidence2Success project (The Social Research Unit, 2012), which looked at the social and emotional well-being of vulnerable children aged 0 to five, examining programmes that target one or more key developmental outcomes in infancy (under two years) and early childhood (three to five years), aiming to achieve positive relationships (reduce risk of maltreatment) and behaviour (increase in pro-social behaviour), emotional well-being (self-regulation and free from depression and anxiety) and educational skills and attainment, particularly readiness for school.

Twenty five of the programmes studied showed positive outcomes and 11 of these were found to be based on strong, reliable evidence. The cost benefits are set out in detail in the Chief Medical Officer's report (Department of Health, 2013; Murphy & Fonagy, 2012). These programmes are currently implemented in the UK primarily through children's centres, child and adolescent mental health services (CAMHS) or other specialist units. They fall into the following five categories:

■ pre-school curricula to enhance children's readiness for school

■ parenting group programmes to improve children's behaviour (eg. Incredible Years)

■ parent and child therapy programmes to improve children's relationships with their parents/carers

- home-visiting programmes to improve children's relationships with their parents/carers (eg. Nurse-Family Partnership)

- intensive child and family support programmes to improve behaviour and children's relationships with their parents/carers/foster parents.

There are a number of other clinically proven and cost-effective interventions. Taking conduct disorder as an example, potential life-long savings from each case prevented through early intervention have been estimated at £150,000 for severe conduct problems and £75,000 for moderate conduct problems (Friedli & Parsonage, 2007).

Challenges

Scarce resources and cuts in public spending have reduced the opportunity for developing and increasing investment in prevention. The Munro review (2011) called for more effective inter-agency working and for empowering social workers with the skills and confidence to act in the best interests of children. Developing effective interventions and services is vital to support neglectful parents. Every community needs to find its own way to shift the investment of public and voluntary sector funding into more early support and prevention.

The 1001 Critical Days Manifesto (Leadsom *et al*, 2013), a cross-party initiative prioritising infant mental health is asking for every baby to receive sensitive and responsive care from their main caregivers in the first years of life. Parents need to feel confident to raise their children in a loving and supportive environment.

A holistic approach to all ante, peri (conception to the first 18 months of life) and postnatal services is sought, which would enable seamless care for all families. This includes midwives, health visitors, GPs and children's centres, and services should engage with families as soon as possible – ideally during pregnancy. The contact that parents have with services before and after the birth of their child provides a unique opportunity to work with them at a stage that is so vitally important to the development of children.

A range of services should be in place in every local area to ensure that women who are at risk or who are suffering from mental health problems are given appropriate support at the earliest opportunity. This includes specialist parent and infant mental health midwives and health visitors trained in this area, to improve identification and support for families who need it most. The availability of specialist perinatal psychiatrists and psychologists who are experts in perinatal care is limited and needs to be better developed across the UK so that every mother with a history of mental health problems can have access to specialist support with a focus on prevention (NICE, 2012).

Every parent should be able to access antenatal classes that address both the physical and emotional aspects of parenthood, as well as the baby's well-being (infant mental health). To enable this to happen, local services must identify and reach families who need additional services.

Maternity services, health visitors, social care, adult mental health services and children's centres who work well together to form a team around a vulnerable mother are important factors in preventing serious mental health problems for mothers and, in turn, new babies. The pooling of budgets to deliver preventative services will encourage innovative commissioning and induce a culture of joined-up working. The early years workforce should receive high-quality training in infant mental health and attachment in order for practitioners to understand parent-infant relationships, and to have a good knowledge of the services required when difficulties arise. Health visitors, midwives, GPs and children's centre staff should be trained to identify the most seriously ill and vulnerable parents.

Joint strategic needs assessment and local health and well-being strategies should cover infant mental health, looking at the consequences in financial and human terms if there is no investment.

Early intervention and the voluntary sector

The voluntary sector can provide important services to new parents. New parents are often comfortable with those who have no statutory duties but who can nevertheless provide support, education and a trusting relationship (see Leadsom *et al*, 2013). Statutory services are increasingly commissioning the voluntary sector and in doing so are broadening the types of services available to vulnerable parents.

Babies in Mind, run by the Mental Health Foundation, is a multidisciplinary and multilevel primary prevention programme, specifically designed to support vulnerable families during the transition to parenthood. After a video is filmed of the mother and baby, mothers are invited to comment on clips about their positive interactions with their infant, thus developing a reflective attitude and greater awareness of the attachment with their baby (Finistrella & Lavis, 2014).

Video Interaction Guidance (VIG) is used in more than 15 countries, is recommended by NICE (2012), and was selected by the NSPCC as one of its two chosen evidence-based interventions to tackle neglect. VIG is used to promote parent-infant interaction, for example through the use of video guidance and access to parent infant psychotherapy, delivered by qualified professionals. An important role for parents is to manage their own emotions and in turn help their baby regulate intense emotions, which can include being inconsolable, fearful and angry.

The Oxford Parent Infant Project (OXPIP) service supports new parents in coping and adapting to the demands of a new baby. A wide range of programmes are offered depending on the needs of parents, including parent/infant psychotherapy, attachment work, VIG, baby massage to promote positive parent-infant interaction, and Watch, Wait and Wonder groups helping mothers to read their babies' cues and soothe them. The organisation helps mothers with depression and anxiety to make the transition to parenting. OXPIP plays an important role in influencing policy makers and commissioners to invest more in early intervention.

Final thoughts

One in 10 British children have mental health problems with indications that this is on the rise. Prevention is more desirable than cure but our current systems are caught in a crisis intervention rather than prevention model. There is strong evidence that we can make a difference by working early with parents, targeting vulnerable families and improving the understanding of attachment and its impact on emotional well-being. Savings can be made for individuals, services and society with this early start.

In order for the UK to move to a culture of prevention from its current emphasis on crisis intervention, a fundamental and new investment in early years services is needed. A joint approach to funding shared across all stakeholders is important to make this shift. Current spending on prevention is low and needs new approaches and innovations to deliver education and to create greater awareness using the internet, social media, parent networks and community groups to ensure the future of the UK's children.

References

Ainsworth M, Bell S & Stayton D (1971) Individual differences in strange situation behavior of one year olds. In: H Schaffer (Ed) *The Origins of Human Social Relations* (pp17–57). London: Academic Press.

Allen G (2011) *Early Intervention: The next steps. An independent report to the Government* [online]. London: DWP & Cabinet Office. Available at: https://www.gov.uk/government/publications/early-intervention-the-next-steps--2 (accessed December 2014).

Balbernie R & Barrows P (2004) *Mental Health in Infancy* [online]. London: YoungMinds. Available at: www.youngminds.org.uk (accessed December 2014).

Dana Corporation (2012) *Reaction to "Equal ≠ the Same: Sex differences in the human brain"* [online]. Available at: dana.org/Cerebrum/ (accessed December 2014).

Department of Health (2013) *Our Children Deserve Better: Prevention pays* [online]. London: DH. Available at: https://www.gov.uk/government/publications/chief-medical-officers-annual-report-2012-our-children-deserve-better-prevention-pays (accessed December 2014).

Finistrella V & Lavis P (2014) Babies in mind: promoting infant mental health. *Journal of Health Visiting* **2** (8) 424–432.

Fraley R, Niedenthal M, Marks M, Brumbaugh C & Vicary A (2006) Adult attachment and the perception of emotional expressions. *Journal of Personality* **74** (4) 1163–90.

Friedli L & Parsonage (2007) *Mental Health Promotion: Building an economic case*. Belfast: Northern Ireland Association for Mental Health.

Grauberg J (2014) *Early Years: Valuable ends and effective means – Centre Forum report July 2014* [online]. Available at: http://www.centreforum.org/index.php/mainpublications/645-early-years (accessed December 2014).

Green H, McGinnity A, Meltzer H, Ford T & Goodman R (2005) *Mental Health of Children and Young People in Great Britain, 2004*. Basingstoke: Palgrave Macmillan.

Leadsom A, Field F, Burstow P & Luca C (2013) *1001 Critical Days* [online]. Available at: http://www.1001criticaldays.co.uk/UserFiles/files/1001_days_jan28_15_final.pdf (accessed April 2015)

Lyons-Ruth K (2008) Contributions of the mother-infant relationship to dissociated and borderline conduct symptoms in young adulthood. *Infant Mental Health Journal* **29** (3) 203–218.

Meins E, Fernyhough C, Arnott B, Leekam S & de Rosnay M (2013) Mind-Mindedness and Theory of Mind: Mediating roles of language and perspectival symbolic play. *Child Development* **84** (5) 1777–1790.

Mikulincer M & Shaver P (2006) *An Attachment Perspective on Interpersonal and Intergroup Conflict* [online]. Available at: www.sydneysymposium.unsw.edu.au/2010/chapters/MikulincerSSSP2010.pdf (accessed December 2014).

Munro E (2011) *The Munro Review of Child Protection: Final report: a child-centred system*. Norwich: The Stationery Office (TSO).

Murphy M & Fonagy P (2012) Mental health problems in children and young people. In: *Our Children Deserve Better: Prevention Pays*. Available at: https://www.gov.uk/government/uploads/system/uploads/attachment_data/file/252660/33571_2901304_CMO_Chapter_10.pdf (accessed December 2014).

NICE (2012) *PH40 Social and Emotional Wellbeing – early years* [online]. London: NICE. Available at: http://www.nice.org.uk/guidance/ph40 (accessed December 2014).

Niedenthal P, Brauer M, Robin L & Innes-Ker Å (2002) Adult Attachment and the Perception of Facial Expression of Emotion. *Journal of Personality & Social Psychology* **82** (3) 419–433.

ONS (1999) *The Mental Health of Children and Adolescents in Great Britain*. London: Office for National Statistics.

Social Research Unit (2012) *Investing in children: Technical report*. Darlington: The Social Research Unit.

Tickell C (2011) *The Early Years: Foundations for life, health and learning* [online]. Available at: https://www.gov.uk/government/collections/tickell-review-reports (accessed December 2014).

Chapter 4: Building resilience and improving mental health and well-being within school settings

By Paula Lavis, Claire Robson and Lily Makurah

There are a number of good reasons why schools should be helping their pupils to be more resilient and mentally healthy. In many crucial ways resilience gives pupils the opportunity to get the most out of their education and prepare for adult life. It helps children and young people to get off to a good start by helping them cope with the stresses and strains they might face in life. It can also help reduce the risk of developing mental health problems and avoid the subsequent impact on the individual, their family, friends and the wider community. The recognition that children and young people need softer skills such as resilience has grown (O'Donnell *et al*, 2014), and the Department for Education have recently added 'Character, Resilience and Grit' as their fifth priority (Whittaker, 2014). If that isn't enough, it can also save schools and key services money.

This chapter is a précis of a briefing written by Public Health England and the Children and Young People's Mental Health Coalition (2015). It considers what resilience and mental health are and the contribution that a 'whole-school approach' can make to building resilience and promoting mental health and well-being in educational settings.

What is mental health?

The World Health Organization defines mental health as:

'… a state of well-being in which the individual realizes his or her own abilities, can cope with the normal stresses of life, can work productively and fruitfully, and is able to make a contribution to his or her community. With respect to children, an emphasis is placed on the developmental aspects, for instance, having a positive sense of identity, the ability to manage thoughts, emotions, as well as to build social relationships, and the aptitude to learn and to acquire an education, ultimately enabling their full active participation in society.'

(WHO, 2014)

There is no one definition of resilience, but it has been referred to as 'the capacity to bounce back from adverse experiences, and succeed despite adversity' (Public Health England & UCL Institute of Health Equity, 2014). Resilience is shaped and built by our experiences, opportunities and relationships. There are four features of resilience:

- Resilience is dynamic and can increase or reduce over time.
- Resilient individuals are not unharmed or invulnerable.
- Highly resilient individuals cannot overcome all adversity.
- There are inequalities in levels of resilience.

(Public Health England & UCL Institute of Health Equity, 2014)

What are the mental health needs of children and young people?

We know that a significant number of children and young people are quite vulnerable and have a high risk of developing, or already have, mental health problems. To put this in context:

- About half a million children and young people in the UK say they are unhappy and dissatisfied with their lives (Children's Society, 2014).
- At least one in 10 children and young people have a diagnosable mental disorder (Green *et al*, 2005).

- One in five fifteen year olds self-harm (Brooks, in press)

- Nearly one in five secondary school children in the UK have been severely abused or neglected during childhood (NSPCC, 2011).

- Thirty-six per cent of children and young people with learning disabilities have a mental health problem, compared with eight per cent of their non-disabled peers (Emerson & Hatton, 2007).

- Seventy-two per cent of children and young people in residential care have some form of emotional and mental health problem (Sempik *et al*, 2008).

- More than 50% of lesbian, gay and bisexual young people deliberately harm themselves (Guasp, 2012).

- Nine out of 10 gypsy, traveller and Roma children experience racist bullying (Lane *et al*, 2014).

- Seventy-five per cent of adult mental health problems begin before the age of 18 (Davies, 2013).

Why schools should be promoting mental health and well-being

Schools have a duty to promote the well-being of their students as formalised in the Education and Inspections Act (2006). The Department for Education's guidance (2014a) recognises that: 'in order to help their pupils succeed, schools have a role to play in supporting them to be resilient and mentally healthy'. Mental health is now included in the *Special Educational Needs and Disability Code of Practice* (Department for Education, 2014b) and says that schools should be looking to identify pupils with possible mental health problems.

Moreover, there is good evidence of the link between pupil health and well-being and attainment (Brooks, 2014). Academic success has a strong positive impact on a child or young person's subjective sense of how good they feel their life is (life satisfaction) and is linked to higher levels of well-being in adulthood (Chanfreau *et al*, 2013). In turn, a child or young person's overall level of well-being will impact on their behaviour and engagement in school and their ability to acquire academic competence in the first place. There is evidence that a well-implemented social and emotional learning programme can significantly improve pupils' attainment by 11 percentage points (Durlak *et al*, 2011).

Children and young people themselves tell us that they want to learn more about how to keep themselves emotionally healthy, as well as learning about specific mental health problems such as eating disorders (Ofsted, 2013).

Schools bear a considerable share of public sector costs for supporting children and young people with poor emotional health and well-being. For instance, it has been estimated that the mean annual costs of educating a pupil are £1,733, but that for pupils with hyperkinetic disorder or ADHD, this figure rises to £2,946. This indicates the costs of additional support from teachers and teaching assistants and other special educational needs provision (Strelitz, 2013; Parsonage *et al*, 2014).

There is therefore a strong economic case for promoting children and young people's emotional health and well-being. Evidence indicates that every £1 spent on social and emotional based programmes in schools provides a total return of nearly £84 (Knapp *et al*, 2011). So while school-based efforts to promote students' mental health and well-being will require more investment, preventative interventions can provide savings by helping children and young people to feel well and to be more resilient, so reducing the need for more costly support.

Whole school approach

This is a whole systems approach: one that goes beyond learning and teaching in the classroom to pervade all aspects of the life of a school including, importantly, the school's ethos and environment and its partnerships with parents/carers and the wider community (Langford *et al*, 2014).

The National Institute for Health and Care Excellence (NICE) has identified a whole school approach as being key to effective practice in promoting social and emotional well-being in both primary and secondary schools (NICE, 2008; NICE, 2009).

Key principles of the whole school approach

Consultation with practitioners[1] has identified that the following principles are helpful in identifying tangible actions that can be embedded within educational settings to promote emotional health and well-being:

■ leadership and management

■ school ethos and environment

---

1   Children and Young People's Mental Health Coalition were commissioned by Public Health England to test the principles with practitioners.

- identifying need, taking evidence-informed action and monitoring impact
- school improvement plan and policies
- learning and teaching
- student voice
- staff development, health and well-being
- working with parents/carers and local communities
- student support services.

Examples of how schools are putting these principles into practice are available on the Children and Young People's Mental Health Coalition's website: www.cypmhc.org.uk.

There is a significant overlap between the key principles of the whole school approach and Ofsted inspection criteria (Ofsted, 2014), and so applying these principles in practice will also have an impact in relation to the key judgement areas of Ofsted inspections.

Leadership and management

All of these key principles are important, but it is essential that emotional health and well-being within the school is led and fully supported by the head, senior management team and governors. This key principle sets the direction for implementing the other principles, which are tangible deliverables that leadership can influence. Evidence demonstrates that support from the senior management team is pivotal to emotional health and well-being initiatives being accepted and embedded within the school (Kendal *et al*, 2013).

There needs to be a champion within the school who can take this work forward. This doesn't have to be the head or a member of the senior management team, but they do need their support.

One of the four key Ofsted judgements includes the quality of leadership in, and management of, the school. Schools have to demonstrate how effectively leadership and management enable all pupils to overcome specific barriers to learning, for example through the effective use of the Pupil Premium and Sports Premium, and the extent to which leaders and managers have created a positive ethos in the school.

School ethos and environment

The learning environment needs to engender a sense of belonging and encourage positive pupil-staff and peer-to-peer relationships. Having a culture that understands the importance of mental health and well-being across the whole school population and that is fully supported by the head and senior management team is a good starting point for setting up relevant initiatives or services within the school.

School improvement plan and policies

The school improvement plan should be based on the current needs of the school and should reflect the importance of promoting emotional health and well-being. The school's policies need to be active documents that support the core business of the school and respond to the needs/changes within the school community. There are some policies that schools must have, including those that address behaviour within the school and supporting pupils with medical conditions (Department for Education, 2014c).

Teaching and learning

The quality of teaching in schools is a key Ofsted judgement area. The inspection criteria (Ofsted, 2014) states that schools should provide a broad and balanced curriculum that meets the needs of all pupils; enables all pupils to achieve their full educational potential and make progress in their learning; and promotes good behaviour, safety, and their spiritual, moral, social and cultural development. Promoting emotional health and well-being through the curriculum will help schools meet these criteria.

Students are more likely to engage in lessons that focus on emotional well-being if they address issues directly relevant to them. These issues will vary depending on what is happening in their personal lives, as well as what is happening at school. So a key task is to think about what some of these issues might be. For example, any transitions such as moving from primary to secondary school, exam stress and planning to go to university are likely to be stressful times for pupils.

Personal, Social and Health Education (PSHE) lessons can be used to actively promote emotional health and well-being, and provide pupils with the skills and knowledge they need to increase their mental and emotional resilience. There are organisations, such as the PSHE Association, that can help schools incorporate emotional health and well-being into PSHE lessons. There are evidence-based programmes, such as the Penn Resilience Programme (PRP), that schools can implement in order to build resilience and promote mental health and well-being within the school.

Mental health and well-being can also be incorporated into the wider curriculum. YoungMinds (2012) have produced some useful videos that suggest some simple and practical ways of incorporating emotional well-being into the curriculum. They suggest simple examples such as having a discussion about a piece of literature or a popular television programme, and using it as a starting point for a discussion about what might be going on inside the mind of a character and how this might influence why they behave in particular ways.

Sport is another way of building resilience and promoting mental health and well-being and has been used by Bacon's College in London alongside other more traditional methods (Youth Sports Trust 2014 Conference, 2014). They have used PE as a tool to engage students and to help them with their other school work. For instance, they use basketball training as a way of learning skills such as teamwork and so on, which can then be used in other lessons. They have a football coach who is also a psychotherapist, who works with students at risk of being excluded from the school and helps them reflect on their work both on the football pitch and in the classroom. To support this work, the school has invested heavily in student support services, which include counsellors, learning mentors, family support workers and a peer mediation team. They also have good links with outside agencies and have set up an 'Integrated Services Panel', which meets weekly to discuss the most vulnerable students. This work has produced some good outcomes and has decreased absences, exclusions and the number of days lost.

Ofsted have a number of good practice case studies on their website. For example, the short video of St Paul's School in Greenwich (Ofsted, 2012), illustrates how the English department is using interesting techniques to encourage students, especially boys, to think about the emotions that are being described in poetry and to communicate these to others.

Student voice

Involving children and young people in important decisions that impact on them helps them to feel part of the school and the wider community, and that they have some control over their lives. But schools don't have to do everything themselves and can find good allies in their local community, such as engaging with local youth parliaments. For example, the St Albans Youth Parliament were concerned about levels of mental health in the district and, supported by staff from Youth Connexions, conducted a survey of 1,800 young people to identify issues faced by pupils in the area. The youth parliament presented their findings to the district council and asked them how they were going to prevent youth suicides. As a result of this, the district council set aside £15,000 of ring-fenced money to deliver stress-reducing and goal-setting workshops in schools that demonstrate why the five ways to well-being (see box 4.1) are so important (Children & Young People's Mental Health Coalition, 2014).

Box 4.1: Five ways to well being

The New Economics Foundation (NEF) (Thompson *et al*, 2008) identified five key elements that have been shown to promote well-being. These are:

- connect
- be active
- take notice
- learning
- giving.

Staff development, health and well-being

As already mentioned, the quality of teaching is a key judgement area for Ofsted (2014). The inspection criteria refers to the importance of ensuring that all teaching staff benefit from appropriate professional development and that performance is rigorously managed. Ensuring that all staff have some training around emotional health and well-being, learn techniques in how to manage difficult behaviours, and become able to identify and signpost students with potential mental health problems, will help their students as well as helping with the school's Ofsted inspections. There are training resources such as MindEd, which is freely available to all (see Resources on p51).

School staff also need to be aware of and supported in relation to their own resilience, mental health and well-being. This is particularly important as school staff can act as positive role models for their students. Demonstrating to pupils how to look after their own health and well-being can't be left to teachers to do in isolation without support from the school. The senior management team and the school's ethos need to be supportive of this approach. They should encourage staff to think about their own emotional health and well-being, and provide relevant training such as mental health first aid.

Identifying need and taking evidence-informed action and measuring impact

A teacher may have a hunch that a student isn't very happy, or is quite distressed, but that is not enough to influence key decisions and actions within a school context.

Some schools, in particular primary schools, use simple approaches to get an idea about how their pupils are feeling each day. For instance, some use simple grading sheets with a smiley face at one end and unhappy face at the other, and ask pupils to indicate how happy or sad they are. This information is then used to help them make an informed decision about whether this is something that needs further exploration and what additional support the child or young person might need.

There are also a number of surveys and questionnaires that have been developed by experts in children and young people's mental health and well-being that can be useful when trying to measure levels of emotional well-being, or to help identify potential mental health difficulties. A good survey or questionnaire will have been tested to ensure that it is reliable and measures what it says it does. Some are easy for schools to use themselves, but others should be used in consultation with a mental health or public health professional working with the school.

As with more informal approaches, these surveys and questionnaires can help schools assess need in a systematic way and make an informed decision about what additional support their pupils need. It can also help address some of the health inequalities that certain groups of pupils may face.

The following are some examples of surveys that could be used to measure levels of well-being:

The Stirling Children's Well-being Scale is a positively worded measure for children aged eight to 15 years.

The Warwick-Edinburgh Mental Well-being Scale (WEMWBS) is also a positively worded measure that can be used with young people aged 13 and over. It is recommended that this scale is used with samples of over 100 people.

As well as measuring well-being, there are also surveys and questionnaires that can help identify potential mental health problems.

The Strengths and Difficulties Questionnaire (SDQ) is an example of a questionnaire that can help identify potential mental health problems. The SDQ is a brief, behavioural screening questionnaire for three to 16 year olds. The Department for Education's guidance on Mental Health and Behaviour in Schools (2014a) refers to the SDQ as a way to help schools judge whether an individual child may have a mental health problem.

Working with parents/carers and local communities

What is happening at home is very important for children and young people's emotional health and well-being. The Ofsted inspection criteria expects schools to be engaging parents in supporting pupils' achievement, behaviour and safety, and their spiritual, moral, social and cultural development. A number of NICE guidance documents point to how important working with parents is for children and young people's emotional health and well-being (NICE, 2008; 2009; 2013a; 2013b; Brown *et al*, 2012).

Some schools work in partnership with child and adolescent mental health services (CAMHS) or other agencies to provide parenting programmes. These are relatively cheap and costs can be recouped within a few years (Parsonage *et al*, 2014). For more information about the importance of parenting programmes, see the Centre for Mental Health's (2014) briefing for schools.

Student support services

Many schools are already working with local agencies such as CAMHS, or are commissioning services to help provide specialist support for their students. These services should be commissioned based on the needs within the school. This is why identifying mental health needs within the school in a systematic way is so important. More information can be found in the full text of the case studies that Public Health England and the Children and Young People's Mental Health Coalition (2015) have produced, or see *Resilience and Results* (Children & Young People's Mental Health Coalition, 2012) for information about how voluntary sector services can help provide specialist support.There is also advice for schools on commissioning mental health and well-being support in the Department for Education's guidance (2014a).

Concluding comments

Promoting the mental health and well-being of staff and pupils is increasingly being recognised as an important and integral part of school effectiveness strategies. This understanding is backed up by evidence showing that emotionally healthy students with higher levels of well-being are more likely to engage with their school, make the most of their education and be prepared for adulthood (Gutman & Vorhaus, 2012; Durlak *et al*, 2011).

A whole school approach provides a useful framework to help schools plan and deliver universal support to promote pupil and staff mental health and well-being in conjunction with other partners. The framework can also be used to demonstrate how actions taken by schools to promote pupils' emotional health and well-being can also help schools meet the Ofsted schools inspection criteria.

Resources

Case studies from the Public Health England and The Children and Young People's Mental Health Coalition – http://www.cypmhc.org.uk/schools_mental_health/

How to Thrive – http://www.howtothrive.org/

Mental Health First Aid England – http://www.mhfaengland.org/

MindEd – https://www.minded.org.uk/

Ofsted Good Practice Case Studies – http://www.ofsted.gov.uk/resources/goodpractice

PSHE Association – https://www.pshe-association.org.uk/

Stirling Children's Well-being Scale – http://www.friendsforlifescotland.org/site/The%20Stirling%20Children's%20Wellbeing%20Scale.pdf

Strengths and Difficulties Questionnaire (SDQ) – http://www.sdqinfo.org/

Warwick-Edinburgh Mental Well-being Scale (WEMWBS) – http://www2.warwick.ac.uk/fac/med/research/platform/wemwbs/swemwbs_7_item.pdf

References

Brooks F (in press) *Report on Self-harming Behaviours in Children and Young People*. St Andrews, Fife: Health Behaviour in School-Aged Children.

Brooks F (2014) *The Link Between Pupil Health and Wellbeing and Attainment: A briefing for head teachers, governors and staff in education settings* [online]. London: Public Health England. Available at: https://www.gov.uk/government/uploads/system/uploads/attachment_data/file/370686/HT_briefing_layoutvFINALvii.pdf (accessed January 2015).

Brown ER, Khan L & Parsons M (2012) *A Chance to Change: Delivering effective parenting programmes to transform lives* [online]. London: Centre for Mental Health. Available at: http://www.centreformentalhealth.org.uk/pdfs/chance_to_change.pdf (accessed January 2015).

Centre for Mental Health (2014) *A Briefing for Schools* [online]. London: Centre for Mental Health. Available at: http://www.centreformentalhealth.org.uk/pdfs/parenting_briefing_schools.pdf (accessed January 2015).

Chanfreau J, Lloyd C, Bryon C, Roberts C, Craig R, De Feo D & McManus S (2013) *Predicting Well-being* [online]. London: NatCen Social Research. Available at: http://www.natcen.ac.uk/our-research/research/predictors-of-wellbeing/ (accessed January 2015).

Children and Young People's Mental Health Coalition (2012) *Resilience and Results: How to improve the emotional and mental wellbeing of children and young people in your school* [online]. London: Children and Young People's Mental Health Coalition. Available at: http://www.cypmhc.org.uk/resources/resilience_results/ (accessed January 2015).

Children and Young People's Mental Health Coalition (2014) *Case Studies* [online]. Available at: http://www.cypmhc.org.uk/resources/?category=13 (accessed January 2015).

Children's Society (2014) *The Good Childhood Report 2014* [online]. London: Children's Society. Available at: http://www.childrenssociety.org.uk/what-we-do/research/well-being-1/good-childhood-report-2014 (accessed January 2015).

Davies SC (2013) *Chief Medical Officer's Annual Report 2012: Our children deserve better: prevention pays* [online]. London: Department of Health. Available at: https://www.gov.uk/government/publications/chief-medical-officers-annual-report-2012-our-children-deserve-better-prevention-pays (accessed January 2015).

Department for Education (2014a) *Mental Health and Behaviour in Schools: Departmental advice for school staff* [online]. London: Department for Education. Available at: https://www.gov.uk/government/uploads/system/uploads/attachment_data/file/326551/Mental_Health_and_Behaviour_-_Information_and_Tools_for_Schools_final_website__2__25-06-14.pdf (accessed January 2015).

Department for Education (2014b) *Special Educational Needs and Disability Code of Practice: 0 to 25 years* [online]. London: Department for Education. Available at: https://www.gov.uk/government/publications/send-code-of-practice-0-to-25 (accessed January 2015).

Department for Education (2014c) *Statutory Policies for Schools* [online]. London: Department for Education. Available at: https://www.gov.uk/government/uploads/system/uploads/attachment_data/file/357068/statutory_schools_policies_Sept_14_FINAL.pdf (accessed January 2015).

Durlak JA, Weissberg RP, Dymnicki AB, Taylor RD & Schellinger KB (2011) The impact of enhancing students' social and emotional learning: a meta-analysis of school-based universal interventions. *Child Development* **82** (1) 405-432.

Emerson E & Hatton C (2007) *The Mental Health of Children and Adolescents with Learning Disabilities in Britain*, Lancaster: Lancaster University. Available at: http://www.lancaster.ac.uk/staff/emersone/FASSWeb/Emerson_07_FPLD_MentalHealth.pdf (accessed January 2015).

Green H, McGinnity A, Meltzer H, Ford T & Goodman R (2005) *Mental Health of Children and Young People in Great Britain, 2004* [online]. London: Palgrave. Available at: http://www.hscic.gov.uk/catalogue/PUB06116/ment-heal-chil-youn-peop-gb-2004-rep1.pdf (accessed January 2015).

Guasp A (2012) *The School Report: The experiences of gay young people in Britain's schools in 2012* [online]. London: Stonewall. Available at: http://www.stonewall.org.uk/documents/school_report_2012(2).pdf (accessed January 2015).

Gutman LM & Vorhaus J (2012) *The Impact of Pupil Behaviour and Wellbeing on Educational Outcomes* [online]. London: Department for Education. Available at: https://www.gov.uk/government/uploads/system/uploads/attachment_data/file/219638/DFE-RR253.pdf (accessed January 2015).

Health Behaviour in School-Aged Children (in press) *Report on Self-harming Behaviours in Children and Young People*. St Andrews, Fife: HBSC.

Kendal S, Keeley P & Callery P (2013) Student help seeking from pastoral care in UK high schools: a qualitative study. *Child and Adolescent Mental Health* **19** (3)178–184.

Knapp M, McDaid D & Parsonage M (Eds) (2011) *Mental Health Promotion and Mental Illness Prevention: The economic case* [online]. London: Department of Health. Available at: https://www.gov.uk/government/uploads/system/uploads/attachment_data/file/215626/dh_126386.pdf (accessed January 2015).

Lane P, Spencer S & Jones A (2014) *Gypsy, Traveller and Roma: Experts by experience* [online]. Chelmsford: Anglia Ruskin University. Available at: http://www.anglia.ac.uk/ruskin/en/home/news/roma_report.Maincontent.0007.file.tmp/Experts%20by%20Experience.pdf (accessed January 2015).

Langford R, Bonell C, Jones H, Pouliou T, Murphy S, Waters E, Komro KA, Gibbs LF, Magnus D & Campbell R (2014) The WHO Health Promoting School framework for improving the health and well-being of students and their academic achievement. *Cochrane Database of Systematic Reviews 2014,* 4 (CD008958).

NICE (2008) *Social and Emotional Wellbeing in Primary Education* [online]. London: NICE. Available at: http://www.nice.org.uk/guidance/PH12 (accessed January 2015).

NICE (2009) *Social and Emotional Wellbeing in Secondary Education* [online]. London: NICE. Avilable at: http://www.nice.org.uk/guidance/ph20 (accessed January 2015).

NICE (2013a) *Social and Emotional Wellbeing for Children and Young People* [online]. London: NICE. Available at: https://www.nice.org.uk/advice/lgb12/resources/non-guidance-social-and-emotional-wellbeing-for-children-and-young-people-pdf (accessed January 2015).

NICE (2013b) A*ntisocial Behaviour and Conduct Disorders in Children and Young People* [online]. London: NICE. Available at: http://www.nice.org.uk/guidance/CG158/chapter/introduction (accessed January 2015).

NSPCC (2011) *Abuse and Neglect: Self-reported sources* [online]. London: NSPCC. Available at: http://www.nspcc.org.uk/globalassets/documents/research-reports/how-safe-children-2014-indicator-06.pdf (accessed January 2015).

O'Donnell G, Deaton A, Durand M, Halpern D & Layard R (2014) *Wellbeing and Policy* [online]. London: Legatum Institute. Available at: http://www.li.com/activities/publications/wellbeing-and-policy (accessed January 2015).

Ofsted (2012) *Good Practice Film – Developing Skills in English: St Paul's School, Greenwich* [film] [online]. London: Ofsted. Available at: https://www.youtube.com/watch?v=TBs4b-pjAuA (accessed January 2015).

Ofsted (2013) *Not Yet Good Enough: Personal, social, health and economic education in schools* [online]. London: Ofsted. Available at: https://www.gov.uk/government/uploads/system/uploads/attachment_data/file/370024/Not_yet_good_enough_personal__social__health_and_economic_education_in_schools_-_report_summary.pdf (accessed January 2015).

Ofsted (2014) *The Framework for School Inspection* [online]. London: Ofsted. Available at: http://www.ofsted.gov.uk/resources/framework-for-school-inspection-january-2012 (accessed January 2015).

Parsonage M, Khan L & Saunders A (2014) *Building a Better Future: The lifetime costs of childhood behavioural problems and the benefits of early intervention* [online]. London: Centre for Mental Health. Available at: http://www.centreformentalhealth.org.uk/pdfs/building_a_better_future.pdf (accessed January 2015).

Public Health England & The Children and Young People's Mental Health Coalition (2015) *Promoting Children and Young People's Emotional Health and Wellbeing: a whole school and college approach*. London: Public Health England. Available at: www.gov.uk/government/publications/promoting-children-and-young-peoples-emotional-health-and-wellbeing.

Public Health England & UCL Institute of Health Equity (2014) *Building Children and Young People's Resilience in Schools. Health Equity Evidence Review 2* [online]. London: Public Health England. Available at: https://www.gov.uk/government/uploads/system/uploads/attachment_data/file/355770/Briefing2_Resilience_in_schools_health_inequalities.pdf (accessed January 2015).

Sempik J, Ward H & Darker I (2008) Emotional and behavioural difficulties of children and young people at entry to care. *Clinical Child Psychology and Psychiatry* **13** (2) 221–233.

Strelitz J (2013) The economic case for a shift to prevention. In: SC Davies (2013) *Annual Report of the Chief Medical Officer 2012: Our children deserve better: prevention pays* [online]. London: Department of Health. Available at: https://www.gov.uk/government/publications/chief-medical-officers-annual-report-2012-our-children-deserve-better-prevention-pays (accessed January 2015).

Thompson S, Aked J, Marks N & Cordon C (2008) *Five Ways to Wellbeing: The evidence* [online]. London: New Economics Foundation. Available at: http://www.neweconomics.org/publications/entry/five-ways-to-well-being-the-evidence (accessed February 2015).

Whittaker F (2014) Moran adds fifth priority for DfE to create well-rounded youngsters. *Academies*

Week **29 September**. Available at: http://academiesweek.co.uk/morgan-adds-fifth-priority-for-dfe-to-create-well-rounded-youngsters/ (accessed January 2015).

WHO (2014) *Mental health action plan 2013–2020* [film] [online]. Geneva: WHO. Available at: http://apps.who.int/iris/bitstream/10665/89966/1/9789241506021_eng.pdf?ua=1 (accessed January 2015).

YoungMinds (2012) *Whole School Emotional Wellbeing* [online]. London: YoungMinds. Available at: http://vimeo.com/40735380 (accessed January 2015).

Youth Sports Trust 2014 Conference (2014) *Health and well-being headteacher discussion* [film] [online]. Available at: https://www.youtube.com/watch?v=oLOEvBsLbZE&list=UUJerWssJeAsbd1kY79oRm7g (accessed January 2015).

Chapter 5: From diagnosis, disease and disorder to decision making, disability and democratic rights – time for a paradigm shift?

By Toby Williamson

Introduction

This chapter considers the limitations and criticisms of traditional mainstream approaches to understanding mental health problems and conditions such as dementia. It also discusses the growing interest in other useful and important ways of understanding mental health problems and dementia – mental capacity, quality of life, and disability – which provide ways of overcoming those limitations and criticisms.

Diagnosing mental health problems

Classification and diagnosis of mental disorders have been fundamental to psychiatry since Emil Kraeplin published his *Compendium der Psychiatrie* in 1883 (Kraeplin, 1883). Kraeplin believed that the main origin of mental health problems ('diseases' by his definition) was biological and genetic malfunction, and the classifications of schizophrenia, bipolar disorder and dementia owe their origin to him. His work represented a significant step away from the crude and often barbaric ways in which people with mental health problems had been treated hitherto and forms the basis of modern psychiatry.

Kraeplin's legacy can be seen in the modern 'bibles' of psychiatry, the American Psychiatric Association's *Diagnostic and Statistical Manual of Mental Disorders* (now in its fifth edition – usually referred to as DSM-5) and the World Health Organization's *International Classification of Mental and Behavioural Disorders*, now in its tenth revision – usually referred to as ICD-10 (American Psychiatric Association, 2013; World Health Organization, 2010). DSM-5 runs to 947 pages and contains 157 disorders (down from 297 in DSM-IV, although the way they have been categorised has changed). These manuals are central to the process of diagnosis, treatment and care for people with mental health problems the world over.

Problems with diagnosis

The process of diagnosing mental health problems, together with selecting appropriate treatments, is a highly contested and politicised area when compared to its equivalent in the field of physical disorders. Unlike most physical disorders, diagnosis continues to rely largely on self-reported symptoms and behaviours, involving a complex range of thoughts, feelings, beliefs, perceptions and cognitive and communication abilities. Pain and distress may not be reported by the individual and they frequently use definitions different to the medical lexicon of 'symptoms', 'illness', 'disorder' or 'disease' to describe their experiences.

This is not to say that diagnosis is of no use; millions of people across the world have found treatments based upon diagnosis to be of great help and some mental health problems and conditions, such as dementia, have a very significant organic component. Yet the more nebulous nature of mental health problems has resulted in many challenges to and criticisms of both the concept and practical utility of classifying and diagnosing mental health problems. These have come from numerous and varied sources, including people experiencing mental health problems, influential thinkers and opinion formers, and mental health professionals, including some psychiatrists. Although these critiques are wide ranging, they have generally focused on a few key areas:

- the negative impact of labelling and medicalising what are deemed to be valid human experiences, even if appearing bizarre or dangerous to the person (and, in a very small minority of cases, to others)

- the often crude, ineffectual, unhelpful and sometimes oppressive forms of care and treatments (including lawful, compulsory detention and treatment) that have been provided

■ the discrimination and exclusion from mainstream society that many people with mental health problems experience as a result of being diagnosed with a mental 'illness'.

(For useful histories and discussions of psychiatry and mental health practice, see Perkins & Repper, 1998; Porter, 2002; Rogers & Pilgrim, 2010.)

Challenges to diagnosis

Although difficult to date, one might argue that since the 1960s growing numbers of alternative approaches have been proposed and sometimes tested, which have challenged the dominance of what historically has been termed the 'medical model' for mental health problems. These have ranged from a wholesale and aggressive rejection of the mental illness paradigm, initiatives led by people with mental health problems to support each other, including, more recently, people with dementia[2], through to more nuanced approaches by mental health services applying concepts such as a 'biopsychosocial' model (Engel, 1977), 'values-based practice' (Woodbridge & Fulford, 2004) or using psychosocial explanations to understand a person's experience (the latter originates well before the 1960s with the work of Sigmund Freud).

These approaches have certainly benefited many individuals. Plenty of people who consider more conventional medical approaches to be important also readily accept that other non-medical interventions can be very effective in reducing distress. Nevertheless, most of these approaches (with some exceptions that have usually been led by 'service users' themselves) tend to remain rooted in concepts of dysfunctions and disorders relating to an individual's health. What has been taken into consideration less, until relatively recently, is adopting a position that attempts to understand people much more in terms of their ability to make decisions about how they live their lives, what a good quality of life means to people, and the way wider society may have to change because its response to people with mental health problems can have a more disabling effect on them than the direct effect of their mental health problems or conditions.

Mental capacity

We each make thousands of decisions every day, and mental capacity means a person's ability to make those decisions. Historically, a diagnosis of a mental

---

2   For examples, see SPK (1993) and the Hearing Voices Network, the National Survivor User Network, and the Dementia Engagement and Empowerment Project (more information in Resources on p64).

health problem or condition has frequently led to people being denied the opportunity to make even the most basic of decisions for themselves, irrespective of their capacity to do so. The regimented, institutionalised care that was a feature of mental health services for so long in most countries (and continues in many countries today) is a prime example of this. Mental health law in the UK took no account of a person's mental capacity and focused on risk, (non) compliance and compulsion instead. And yet, while mental health problems and conditions such as dementia may affect a person's ability to make a decision, so too can some physical health problems, intoxication and the influence of others.

This situation has changed significantly over the last 15 years in the UK, and this provides a different approach to some of the challenges outlined above. Mental health law is rarely used for people with dementia (or other cognitive disabilities) as compared to so-called 'functional' mental health problems (psychosis etc.), yet until relatively recently there was no clear legal framework to protect a person's right to make decisions whenever possible, or for others to make decisions on their behalf when necessary. This changed in Scotland with the introduction of the Adults with Incapacity (Scotland) Act (2000) and in England and Wales in 2007 when the Mental Capacity Act (2005) came into force[3].

Mental capacity legislation

Although the Scottish and English/Welsh laws are quite different in many respects, they still marked a very important step in the development of positive legal rights and a more progressive approach to how both mental health services and society more widely should respond to people with mental health problems and conditions. Although both have sets of principles, we will focus on the Mental Capacity Act (MCA) rather than the Scottish legislation, as these are, on the face of it, more far reaching. Box 5.1 sets out the five principles of the MCA[4].

It is particularly important to focus on the first three principles, which emphasise the right of people to make decisions for themselves as the starting point in any given situation, irrespective of any illness, disability or condition. People should be provided with as much support as possible to make decisions for themselves (particularly important for people with dementia and learning disabilities), and what may be perceived to be an 'unwise' decision by others (difficult though this may often be to define) should not be taken as evidence of a lack of capacity. The act goes on to describe how a person's capacity to make a decision should be assessed and the process for making a 'best interests' decision on behalf of someone who lacks the capacity to make the decision for themselves.

---

3   At the time of writing, Northern Ireland is considering how to create a new law combining both mental health and mental capacity.

4   See Resources on p64 for official guidance on how the MCA should be used in practice.

Box 5.1: The five principles of the Mental Capacity Act (2005)

- Presumption of capacity – a person should always be presumed to have capacity unless it is proved otherwise.

- Supported decision making – a person should not be considered to be lacking capacity to make a decision until all practicable efforts to help them have been tried.

- Unwise decisions – a person should not be considered to be lacking capacity to make a decision just because they are making an unwise decision.

- Best interests – any decision or action taken on behalf of a person who lacks capacity to make the decision must be done in their best interests.

- Less restrictive option – before the decision is made or the action taken, consideration should be given to whether it can be done in a way that is less restrictive of the person's basic rights and freedoms.

The MCA applies to virtually any decision, great or small, in a person's life. It emphasises that mental capacity is decision- and time-specific (a person may be unable to make one decision at a moment in time but this should not be seen as proof of never being able to make the decision, or not being able to make other decisions). A person's capacity or their best interests should not be judged based solely on their age, appearance, behaviour or condition, and the act emphasises the importance of consulting with others who know the person, especially when making best interests decisions. The act also provides ways in which people can plan ahead for a time when they may not have capacity, establishes a statutory right to advocacy for the first time, and provides other important legal safeguards. A code of practice explains how the act should be used in everyday practice (Office of the Public Guardian, 2013).

The MCA is vitally important in many ways for people with mental health problems and conditions. Application of the act has numerous positive benefits and underpins many processes that remain central to mental health care, treatment and support, because all of these have decision-making at the heart of them, by service users primarily, but others as well. A service user's experience of consent to care, treatment and support, care planning, personalisation, recovery approaches, the 'choice and control' agenda, safeguarding and risk management (including positive risk taking) should all benefit from the MCA being used correctly, in a way that supports them to make their own decisions whenever possible.

The MCA doesn't negate the need in some situations to use compulsory powers, although it is recognised that the interface with the Mental Health Act (2007) (MHA) can be complicated (Williamson & Daw, 2013). Additional safeguards were introduced for people lacking capacity who are detained in hospitals and care homes but not covered by the MHA – the Deprivation of Liberty Safeguards (DoLS). Despite the fact that the MCA has been warmly welcomed by many, including mental health professionals, it has been disappointing that awareness, understanding and compliance with the act have been found lacking in some settings (Williams *et al*, 2012a; 2012b; House of Lords Select Committee on the Mental Capacity Act 2005, 2014). Some mental health services still pay insufficient regard to the MCA as compared to the MHA, especially in situations where people are compulsorily detained and treated under the MHA – the MCA still applies to all decisions except those in relation to a person's care and treatments that are authorised by the MHA.

Although legislation is critically important in establishing an individual's rights, the concept of mental capacity has in its own right the potential to go further than this through changing culture as well as structures. Focusing on a person's ability to make decisions rather than symptoms can still take into account the effects of a mental health problem, however one defines it. But, in addition to this, if applied positively in the way that mental capacity legislation directs one, it also has the potential to create far more respectful, supportive, collaborative and empowering relationships between service users and those who are involved in their care and support.

Quality of life

Decision-making is also central when considering what makes for a good quality of life. Defining and measuring quality of life is a notoriously difficult thing to do and is inevitably affected by an individual's subjective experience (see, for example, Alzheimer's Society, 2010). Where there has been a belief in the efficacy of 'cures' for mental health problems and conditions, quality of life has not been seen as so important because it has usually been assumed that a good quality of life will replace a poorer quality of life once the cure or treatment successfully addresses the health problem.

Yet the shortcomings and unpleasant side effects of many medical treatments for people diagnosed with 'illnesses' such as schizophrenia, and the failure to find any universally effective treatments for dementia, let alone a cure, has brought quality of life issues increasingly into play. Initiatives started mainly by service users, such as the recovery approach and self-management, contain an acknowledgement that, for some people, mental distress, hearing voices, having bizarre beliefs and many other 'symptoms' of mental health problems are experiences they may live with on a day-to-day basis for a large part of their life.

Having some measure of control over these experiences while also being able to maximise quality of life (which heavy duty sedative antipsychotics often don't allow) is therefore crucial, but this is much wider than just a health issue.

Maintaining good physical health, having positive meaningful relationships, being able to participate in the wider community through work or other activities, having a safe and secure place to live and adequate income, and being free from harassment and discrimination can all be as important as managing one's mental health. This was recognised perhaps most significantly with the publication of the Labour government's Social Exclusion Unit (SEU) report on mental health (Social Exclusion Unit, 2004). It was arguably the furthest that government has ever reached in acknowledging the limitations of a more traditional medical (or even biopsychosocial) approach to mental health problems, and the importance of addressing stigma and discrimination, employment, housing and opportunities for community participation. The economic crisis of 2008, the austerity measures that followed, and a change of government and ideology in 2010, somewhat dashed the aspirations contained in the report.

In the case of dementia, an increasing number of people are diagnosed earlier in the progression of the condition but then find they may have to live with the condition for many years without any effective medical interventions to help them. While this may eventually change depending upon research into cure and treatments, psychological and social interventions are playing an increasingly important role in helping many people to maximise their quality of life and to 'live well' with dementia. However, the search for a health intervention that will permanently halt or reverse all the different forms of the condition may simply take too long. The current focus on 'dementia-friendly communities' is a partial indicator of this, involving policy and practice moving beyond the traditional confines of health and social care services for people living with dementia and seeking to change the attitudes and behaviours in the wider community (Alzheimer's Society, 2010; Department of Health, 2012; Joseph Rowntree Foundation, 2014; Local Government Association, 2012). However, the emphasis has tended to focus more on raising awareness of dementia within communities and enabling them to be more supportive of people with dementia, rather than the more structural changes proposed in the social exclusion report (Social Exclusion Unit, 2004).

Interestingly, there is no substantial evidence associating poorer quality of life with a diagnosis of dementia, although this may not be the experience of individuals' close family carers, or their experience in the later stages of dementia (Woods, 2012). Reviews of the literature around quality of life and dementia also suggest that positive coping styles may enable people to adapt well to living with dementia, in the same way that studies have shown that people with other long-term conditions have done (Alzheimer's Society, 2010). There is certainly evidence of poorer quality of life and emotional well-being for people who have dementia and depression, a common combination which it is estimated may affect up to 50% of people living with dementia, but this would suggest that the priority might be to address a person's depression.

Disability

In some respects, therefore, one can argue that at least some long-term and severe mental health problems (or the experience of living with them) and dementia are much more akin to living with a long-term physical condition or disability. This is not, however, intended to paint a picture of hopelessness or fatalism for two main reasons. First, the majority of people do recover from episodes of mental distress for a variety of different reasons. And second, evidence shows that people can live positive and fulfilling lives with long-term conditions and disabilities providing they receive the support and acceptance that they require, and that societal changes occur that enable this to happen.

Social model of disability

This is moving towards a position that views mental health problems and conditions through the the 'social model of disability'. Largely developed and promoted by people with disabilities (initially physical and learning disabilities), this understands a health problem that has disabling effects not as something that exists solely at the level of the individual, but as an outcome produced by wider social processes of exclusion that stigmatise, discriminate and 'blame' the person with the disability for their situation. Changes therefore need to be made in wider society to accommodate people with disabilities, rather than trying to change the disability so people fit in with society. People with disabilities are viewed as citizens with the same rights as anyone else, and the focus should be on their skills and aspirations rather than their deficits. Changes to employment, housing, transport, the built environment and the attitudes of non-disabled people become the main objective.

Using a social model of disability for mental health problems and dementia has gained support over recent years from a number of sources (Barnes & Mercer, 2004; Beresford, 2005; Mulvany, 2000). The Social Exclusion Unit report (2004) and dementia-friendly community initiatives can be seen as practical evidence of this, but equality and human rights legislation provide clearer evidence of the influence the model is having. Kitwood's concepts of malignant social psychology and personhood in the field of dementia are also relevant in this context (Kitwood, 1997).

Equality legislation

The Equality Act (2010) (covering the whole of the UK) replaced the Disability Discrimination Act (1995) and includes provisions that ban discrimination on the grounds of disability as well as requiring 'reasonable adjustments' to be made to ensure organisations, services, businesses, employers and the public environment are made accessible to people with disabilities. The Equality Act defines disability as having a physical or mental impairment that has a 'substantial' and 'long-term' negative effect on a person's ability to do normal daily activities. The UK is also a signatory to the 2006 United Nations Convention on the Rights of Persons with Disabilities (CRPD), which aims to protect the human rights and dignity of people with disabilities. This explicitly adopts a social model of disability and defines disability as including 'those who have long-term physical, mental, intellectual or sensory impairments which in interaction with various barriers may hinder their full and effective participation in society on an equal basis with others'.

The implications of the Equality Act and the CRPD are potentially very significant for people with mental health problems and conditions. Making buildings wheelchair-accessible can be a costly business but very tangible in effect. Ensuring that services and environments are accessible and non-discriminatory for people with mental health problems or dementia is more challenging and it is difficult to identify the full range of actions it may entail. The law is yet to be widely tested in these areas and particularly for dementia (especially in relation to the later stages of the condition) and there is little recognition to date of it constituting a disability as defined by law. Yet a growing body of evidence to indicate that changes in the physical environments of buildings (eg. signage, use of colour) can reduce cognitive confusion for people living with dementia may mean that 'dementia-friendly' becomes 'dementia-accessible' and required by law. With the UK being required by the United Nations to report its compliance with the CRPD in 2016 (interestingly, the MCA is probably not compliant with the CRPD, partly because the latter places a much greater emphasis on supported decision making), it is quite possible that the social model of disability may need to become more widely understood and incorporated into policy and practice for people with mental health problems and dementia.

Conclusion

Mental health problems and dementia are very real and often very distressing for the individual experiencing them. Yet right up to the current day, processes of diagnosis, care and treatment have proved less straightforward than in physical illnesses, and have been experienced by many as unwarranted, unwanted, unhelpful or oppressive.

Mental capacity, quality of life and disability provide alternative paradigms for thinking about and understanding mental health problems and conditions. While still acknowledging the distress and cognitive difficulties mental health problems and dementia may cause, these models have a number of additional benefits including:

- a wider and more inclusive view of the impact they have on people's lives

- legal frameworks that have a strong focus on empowerment and support

- a greater onus for society as a whole to make adjustments to support people and enable them to live well with a mental health problem or dementia.

Understanding the importance of decision-making and quality of life is something we should all be capable of, and if society increasingly recognises physically disabled people as people first and a disability second, isn't it time we did the same with people with mental health problems and dementia? The law certainly suggests we do.

Resources

Alzheimer's Society – dementia-friendly communities: http://www.alzheimers.org.uk/site/scripts/documents_info.php?documentID=1843

Dementia Engagement and Empowerment Project (DEEP): http://www.dementiavoices.org.uk/

Hearing Voices Network: http://www.hearing-voices.org/

Joseph Rowntree Foundation – dementia-friendly communities: http://www.jrf.org.uk/topic/dementia-without-walls

Local Government Association – dementia-friendly communities: http://www.local.gov.uk/web/guest/ageing-well/what-makes/-/journal_content/56/10180/3489459/ARTICLE

Mental Capacity Act: https://www.gov.uk/government/collections/mental-capacity-act-making-decisions

National Survivor User Network: http://www.nsun.org.uk/

References

Alzheimer's Society (2010) *My Name is Not Dementia: Literature review*. London: Alzheimer's Society.

American Psychiatric Association (2013) *Diagnostic and Statistical Manual of Mental Disorders, 5th Edition*. Arlington, VA: APA.

Barnes C & Mercer G (Eds) (2004) *Implementing the Social Model of Disability: Theory and research*. Leeds: Disability Press.

Beresford P (2005) Developing self-defined social approaches to distress. In: S Ramon and J Williams (Eds) *Mental Health at the Crossroads: The promise of the psychosocial approach*. London: Ashgate.

Department of Health (2012) *The Prime Minister's Challenge on Dementia* [online]. London: Department of Health. Available at: https://www.gov.uk/government/publications/prime-ministers-challenge-on-dementia (accessed January 2015).

Department of Health (2015) *Prime Minister's Challenge on Dementia 2020* [online]. London: Department of Health. Available at: https://www.gov.uk/government/publications/prime-ministers-challenge-on-dementia-2020 (accessed February 2015).

Engel GL (1977) The need for a new medical model: a challenge for biomedicine. *Science* **196** (4286) 129–136.

House of Lords Select Committee on the Mental Capacity Act 2005 (2014) *Mental Capacity Act 2005: Post-legislative scrutiny. Report of Session 2013–14*. HL Paper 139 [online]. London: SO. Available at: http://www.publications.parliament.uk/pa/ld201314/ldselect/ldmentalcap/139/139.pdf (accessed January 2015).

Joseph Rowntree Foundation (2014) *Dementia Without Walls* [online]. York: Joseph Rowntree Foundation. Available at: http://www.jrf.org.uk/topic/dementia-without-walls (accessed January 2015).

Kitwood T (1997) *Dementia Reconsidered: The person comes first*. Buckingham: Open University Press.

Kraeplin E (1883) *Compendium der Psychiatrie*.

Local Government Association (2012) *Developing Dementia-friendly Communities: Learning and guidance for local authorities* [online]. London: Local Government Association. Available at: http://www.local.gov.uk/c/document_library/get_file?uuid=b6401bb0-31a8-4d57-823b-1fde6a09290e&groupId=10180 (accessed January 2015).

Mulvany J (2000) Disability, impairment or illness? The relevance of the social model of disability to the study of mental disorder. *Sociology of Health and Illness* **22** (5) 582–601.

Office of the Public Guardian (2013) *Mental Capacity Act Code of Practice* [online]. Available at: https://www.gov.uk/government/publications/mental-capacity-act-code-of-practice (accessed January 2015).

Perkins R & Repper J (1998) *Dilemmas in Community Mental Health Practice*. Abingdon: Radcliffe Medical Press.

Porter R (2002) *Madness: A brief history*. Oxford: Oxford University Press.

Rogers A & Pilgrim D (2010) *A Sociology of Mental Health and Illness*. Maidenhead: Open University Press.

Social Exclusion Unit (2004) *Mental Health and Social Exclusion*. London: Office of the Deputy Prime Minister.

SPK (1993) *Turn Illness Into a Weapon*. Heidelberg: KRRIM – self-publisher for illness.

Williams V, Boyle G, Jepson M, Swift P, Williamson T & Heslop P (2012a) *Making Best Interests Decisions: People and processes* [online]. London: Mental Health Foundation. Available at: http://www.mentalhealth.org.uk/content/assets/PDF/publications/BIDS_report_24-02-12_FINAL1.pdf?view=Standard (accessed January 2015).

Williams V, Boyle G, Jepson M, Swift P, Williamson T & Heslop P (2012b) *Making Best Interests Decisions: People and processes*. Appendices A–F. London: Mental Health Foundation. Available at: http://www.mentalhealth.org.uk/content/assets/PDF/publications/BIDs_appendices_FINAL.pdf?view=Standard (accessed January 2015).

Williamson T & Daw R (2013) *Law, Values and Practice in Mental Health Nursing: A handbook*. Maidenhead: Open University Press.

Woodbridge K & Fulford KWM (2004) *Whose Values? A workbook for values in mental health care*. London: Sainsbury Centre for Mental Health.

Woods B (2012) Well-being and dementia: how can it be achieved? *Quality in Ageing and Older Adults* **13** (3) 205–211.

World Health Organization (2010) *International Classification of Mental and Behavioural Disorders, 10th Edition*. Geneva: WHO.

Chapter 6: What is 'parity of esteem'? Is it a useful concept?

By Emily Wooster

'Parity: 1. *Equality, equal status or pay etc.*
             2. *Being valued at par*

Esteem: *To think highly of. To consider or regard'*

(*Oxford English Dictionary*, 1989)

Introduction

'Parity of esteem' is a recently coined phrase that refers to treating mental health equally with physical health. Its origins lie in the Health and Social Care Act (2012) where, at the time of the passage of the legislation, organisations and lobby groups fought for explicit reference to mental health as well as physical health. Of course, for many years charities have questioned the lack of equality in mental health – the first report for the We Need to Talk coalition (a coalition working for better access to psychological therapies on the NHS) said in 2006:

'A failure to offer evidence based treatments for physical health problems like cancer would lead to a national outcry. We believe the non-availability of psychological therapies is equally unacceptable.'

(Bird, 2006, p2)

The principle that has come to be known as 'parity of esteem' is now frequently used by politicians, and has begun to infiltrate the media.

The desire to enshrine the parity principle into law and make explicit reference to mental health (while setting it apart from physical health) shows that it is recognised that mental health has not been on an equal footing in the past. Mental health is still very much the 'loser' in the health system in comparison to physical health – it is poorly understood and poorly funded considering the numbers of people experiencing mental ill-health, and there is very little available for those who are suffering. A stark health inequality is that people with severe mental health problems have a life expectancy reduced by 20 years compared to that of the general population, with the vast majority of these deaths being 'avoidable' (Rethink Mental Illness, 2013). It is hard to imagine any other area of healthcare where this would be acceptable. People with mental ill-health experience stigma and discrimination in the health service, in employment, in education and in the wider community. And despite the rhetoric around moving towards parity, there has been little progress in that direction.

This chapter discusses some of the recent policy changes that have hampered the move towards parity of esteem and questions how comparing mental health to physical health may sometimes be problematic.

Recommendations from the parity working group

Following on from the UK government's commitment to parity, work was carried out by an expert working group set up by the Care Services Minister to define 'parity of esteem' in detail – ie. to examine why parity between mental health and physical health does not currently exist and how it might be achieved in practice. The working group was made up of key experts in the field including service users, professionals, voluntary sector workers and academics.

Recommendations from the working group included:

- funding services, ensuring research and treatments are commensurate to need

- developing access standards and improving waiting times for mental health, which have long been poor in comparison to physical health with people having to wait months, sometimes years, for access to some treatments

- tackling stigma and discrimination – for example, operating a 'zero tolerance' approach to stigma in health and social care settings

- measures to address the premature mortality of people with mental health problems.

The working group considered the importance of services taking a life-course approach to mental health, which would mean ensuring that older people and children and young people are supported equally to working age adults. The group also considered parity within mental health – ie. addressing the inequalities (which could be social, economic and/or health related) experienced by certain groups who are also more likely to experience mental ill-health, such as people with complex needs, black and minority ethnic communities, refugees and asylum seekers, people with learning disabilities, and those who are homeless. Addressing parity within mental health would mean adapting our services and making adjustments – for example, adapting psychological support so it can reach older people in the home or ensuring that steps are taken to ensure therapy is culturally appropriate (Royal College of Psychiatrists, 2013).

Where we are now

The report from the parity working group set out a clear road map on how progress towards parity of esteem could be made in health and social care (Royal College of Psychiatrists, 2013). However, although progress towards a more equal health system was never going to happen overnight, some recent policy decisions have seemingly undermined attempts to address parity.

Funding

Perhaps the most obvious example of the government not redressing inequalities between mental and physical health is the recent decisions made over funding cuts in mental health. It has long been understood that mental health has been underfunded; only 13% of the NHS budget goes on mental health, despite mental ill-health representing 23% of all ill-health in the UK – the largest single cause of disability (London School of Economics, 2012). Earlier this year, NHS England and the health regulator Monitor cut funding for mental health and other community services by 20% more than NHS hospital trusts – a decision made to account for delivery of the Francis recommendations and report following the public inquiry into the failings at Mid Staffordshire NHS Foundation Trust. This attracted widespread criticism at the time because, on the one hand, there had been a commitment to address funding, and on the other, because services were being cut, and proportionately more so than other services (Mental Health Policy Group, 2014).

This year, therefore, Monitor and NHS England are looking to apply the same cuts across the board, 'equally' to mental health and physical health – however, this will not achieve parity either. To achieve equality, sometimes you even have to treat something or someone differently so that it might become 'more equal', to achieve that level playing field – this principle is enshrined in equalities legislation, too. In these current austere times, mental health services being 'equally cut' to other health services does not go far enough to address the inequality of funding.

Treatment and support

Until the 1950s there were very few treatment options for people with mental ill-health beyond pharmacological treatments such as antipsychotics and antidepressants. In the 1970s psychological therapies started to be developed and trialled. Today, a number of different treatments are recommended including psychological therapies for a range of mental health diagnoses, mindfulness-based cognitive therapy (for those with recurrent depression) and exercise. However, in reality these can still be hard to access through the health service. For example, a recent report by the We Need to Talk coalition found that one in five people were still waiting for over a year to access them (Mind, 2013). Mindfulness and exercise on prescription are also difficult to access on the NHS and through social care, although employers and schools are beginning to think about people more broadly, in the knowledge that these approaches have benefits for organisations as well as individuals in terms of helping people's attention to detail, focus, reducing anxiety and improving well-being.

The government is introducing access standards and waiting times as of April 2015, which should mean that people do not have to wait for so long to access psychological therapies, but whether this will lead to the expansion of a broader range of treatments, particularly in primary care (where the vast majority of people with mental problems are supported), remains to be seen. A real challenge is still attitudinal and convincing professionals and commissioners about what works for supporting people with mental health problems. Similarly, the expansion of things such as debt advice, housing support and relationship counselling for people with mental ill-health is critically important.

Inequalities

Parity within mental health means recognising that certain groups experience health inequalities as well as social and economic inequalities. Often these things go hand-in-hand and a complex and diverse set of circumstances will create or exacerbate mental distress, including poverty, lack of access to social support, violence and trauma or relationship and familial problems. Certain population groups are also more at risk of developing mental health problems – those living in poverty, people who are homeless or at risk of homelessness, people with learning disabilities and refugees and asylum seekers, to name a few. Often those most at risk of developing mental health problems are also poorly served by services and support.

A life-course approach to mental health means giving equal (or even more) support to the mental health needs of children and young people and older people too (see Chapters 3, 4 and 9). While this may seem obvious, in reality there has been a focus on supporting the mental health and well-being of the economically productive ('working age' adults) – for example, the legacy of the government's flagship Improving Access to Psychological Therapy (IAPT) scheme is that, up until recently, it supported 'working age' adults only.

There has been less investment in services for children and young people, and while the government is now beginning to roll-out IAPT services for this group, local authority cuts mean there has been huge disinvestment in well-being and prevention work in children and young people's mental health services. A recent Freedom of Information request by the charity YoungMinds demonstrated that more than half of councils had cut or frozen budgets for child and adolescent mental health (YoungMinds, 2014).

The funding gap for older adult mental health services is large. It was estimated in 2008 that around £2 billion of additional funding would be required to eliminate the inequality in service provision between middle-aged people (defined as those aged 35–54) and people aged 55 or over (Beecham *et al*, 2008, in Royal College of Psychiatrists, 2013). Older people are more likely to experience isolation and may find it difficult to access services due to their physical disabilities, self-stigma or because of discriminatory attitudes that being low or anxious is 'just part of getting old'.

The mortality gap

Life expectancy for people with mental ill-health is, on average, between 15–20 years earlier than the general population, with the mortality gap largely due to preventable physical health problems such as cardiovascular disease, diabetes and stroke. Mortality rates have been attributed to a number of factors, including weight gain caused by side effects of antipsychotics, and smoking, which is much more prevalent among people with mental health problems. An inquiry by the Disability Rights Commission as early as 2006 showed that people with mental ill-health often have their physical health symptoms overlooked or even attributed to their mental ill-health – known as 'diagnostic overshadowing' which leads to health professionals delaying diagnosis and treatment (Disability Rights Commission, 2006).

A recent study of Nordic countries published in the *British Journal of Psychiatry* confirmed that the mortality gap between those with mental ill-health and the general population has not changed over the past 20 years. Graham Thornicroft, Professor of Community Psychiatry at the Institute of Psychiatry, described the findings in the journal's editorial as a 'scandal' and said, 'If such a disparity in mortality rates affected a less stigmatised section of the population … then we would witness an outcry' (Thornicraft, 2011).

One way of redressing this is through health checks, and GPs have been incentivised through the quality outcomes framework (or QOF) to provide these to people with a diagnosis of schizophrenia, bipolar or psychosis. This year a large number of indicators were removed from the QOF (not just mental health indicators) including indicators related to monitoring blood glucose, cholesterol and body mass index for people with severe mental health problems. Those that negotiated the changes insist that there is no expectation that GPs will stop conducting these health checks in their practices.

The mortality gap for people with mental ill-health illustrates entrenched stigmatising attitudes and a disregard for people's health that needs urgently addressing. The Mental Health Policy Group (a lobbying group made up of some of the largest national mental health charities) are lobbying for a national, measurable reduction in the mortality gap.

Is parity a helpful concept?

Mental health is, of course, different to physical health – if you have a broken leg, this can be easily diagnosed by an x-ray and then treated, but being mentally unwell is a subjective experience that affects the way we think, feel and behave. Mental health diagnosis relies much more on self-reporting, with some diagnoses given by health professionals being controversial and much contested with people often treated according to their label. Symptoms of mental health problems include such things as low mood, anxiety or panic (which are often seen as more extreme or negative versions of the everyday experiences that we all have) and less common symptoms such as hearing, smelling or seeing things (hallucinations). While some people like to receive a diagnosis, others are uncomfortable with it, or may refuse treatment altogether. A really key difference between mental health and physical health is that you can be detained against your will if a professional decides that you are 'mentally unwell'. So would people with mental ill-health be better supported through other means (ie. support other than what is provided by the health service)?

Certainly the answers don't lie in the health system alone, and some would say they don't lie in the health service at all. Reasons for mental ill-health are complex – poor attachment or childhood trauma, poverty, losing a job or a relationship breakdown can all lead us to become unwell. It is widely thought that childhood trauma makes people more susceptible to mental health problems, while life experiences also make us more vulnerable. Perhaps it is more helpful, then, to think of parity of esteem in mental health as being about parity in all aspects of our lives. The steps we can take to address this might include looking at wider fiscal policies and the social determinants of mental health, as well as a focus on families and early intervention. The parity working group talked about the need for the government to look at the wider policy agenda of welfare reform, employment and education in improving parity, although the subsequent focus has very much been on the role of the health service (and occasionally social care) in addressing it.

Pervasive, stigmatising attitudes have also affected, and continue to affect, our response to mental ill-health, including the under-funding of services, the provision of treatment and support, and the lack of progress in addressing the mortality gap. We need to ensure that stigma remains on the agenda and features in any discussions about addressing parity in mental health.

Reform in mental health is long overdue and very much needed. There has been huge progress in our understanding of mental health, mental ill-health and in our response to it. The expansion of psychological therapies, the effect of anti-stigma campaigns such as Time to Change and recent policy initiatives such as the introduction of waiting times will change public attitudes towards mental health, and people's experiences of being supported.

However, linking mental health so closely to physical health raises challenges – mental health is not just the responsibility of the health and social care system. In our attempt to address mental health 'equality' we mustn't take a too reductive or narrow focus, where we default to the health and social care system – after all, we have fought for so long to ensure a wider and better understanding of mental health.

References

Beecham J, Knapp M, Fernández J, Huxley P, Mangalore R, McCrone R, Winter B & Witteberg R (2008) *Age Discrimination in Mental Health Services. Personal Social Services Research Unit: discussion paper 2536* [online]. Personal Social Services Research Unit. Available at: https://kar.kent.ac.uk/13344/1/dp2536.pdf (accessed January 2015).

Bird A (2006) *We Need to Talk: Getting the right therapy at the right time*. London: Mind.

Disability Rights Commission (2006) *Equal Treatment: Closing the gap* [online]. Available at: http://disability-studies.leeds.ac.uk/files/library/DRC-Health-FI-main.pdf (accessed January 2015).

London School of Economics (2012) *Why Mental Health Loses Out* [online]. London: London School of Economics and Political Science. Available at: http://cep.lse.ac.uk/pubs/download/special/cepsp26.pdf (accessed January 2015).

Mental Health Policy Group (2014) Risk of deep cuts in mental health funds. *The Guardian* **12 March**. Available at: http://www.theguardian.com/society/2014/mar/12/risks-deep-cuts-mental-health (accessed January 2015).

Mind (2013) *We Need to Talk: Getting the right therapy at the right time*. London: Mind.

Oxford English Dictionary (1989) Oxford: Oxford University Press.

Rethink Mental Illness (2013) *Lethal Discrimination: Why people with mental health problems are dying needlessly and what needs to change*. London: Rethink Mental Illness.

Royal College of Psychiatrists (2013) *Parity of Esteem – Whole-person Care: From rhetoric to reality (achieving parity between mental and physical health)*. London: Royal College of Psychiatrists.

Thornicroft G (2011) Physical health disparities and mental illness: the scandal of premature mortality (Editorial). *The British Journal of Psychiatry* **199** (6) 441–442.

YoungMinds (2014) *Devastating Cuts Leading to Children's Mental Health Crisis* [online]. London: YoungMinds. Available at: http://www.youngminds.org.uk/news/news/2094_devastating_cuts_leading_to_childrens_mental_health_crisis (accessed January 2015).

Chapter 7: Mental health and work

By Andy Bell

Introduction

At any one time, one in four of us will be experiencing a mental health condition, most often depression or anxiety. Mental ill-health affects people of all ages and in every workplace, big or small. It is a reality of life that we too often sweep under the carpet, and we do so at a great price.

The costs of mental health conditions to UK workplaces are estimated to be at least £26 billion across the economy, or £1,000 per employee per year (see Figure 7.1). The largest proportion of these costs is due to 'presenteeism', where people are at work but are underperforming due to ill-health, while just under a third is due to sickness absence (Centre for Mental Health, from Sainsbury Centre, 2007).

Figure 7.1: The cost of mental health conditions

£95

£335

£605

Total cost: £1,035

- sickness absence
- reduced productivity at work
- staff turnover

(Centre for Mental Health, from Sainsbury Centre, 2007)

Despite their prevalence, awareness of mental health conditions in workplaces in the UK is remarkably low. Most employers under-estimate how common mental ill-health is and do not recognise the impact it has on their business. Many do not believe they even employ someone with a mental health problem, or they fear that someone with depression will be hard to manage or unreliable.

Only a quarter of people who have depression receive any treatment for it, and as a result they stay ill for longer at great cost to themselves and their employers.

Too often work is seen as a threat to our health and something to avoid if you have a mental health problem. 'Stress' is sometimes seen as an illness in itself. People with mental health conditions are signed off sick by their doctors for fear they could not cope with work. Many never return. Too often they lose touch with work because colleagues don't know what to say to them. The result is a loss of livelihood for the individual and the loss of a valuable employee for the business.

Yet the evidence suggests that, on the whole, good work is good for both mental and physical health and having a job can be an important part of a recovery journey (Waddell & Burton, 2006). For most people with depression or anxiety, being in work helps them to recover and even very simple steps can make the difference between staying at work and going off sick. Organisations that manage mental health at work proactively, such as BT, have found that about 30% of the cost can be saved, most visibly in reduced sickness absence.

This chapter looks at three important aspects of the relationship between workplaces and mental health and what the evidence says about the interventions that make a difference.

Prevention and early intervention

Creating the conditions for a happy, productive workforce to function at its best can take many approaches. A lot of large employers in the UK are signed up to programmes to promote employee well-being that have both mental and physical aspects, and there is good evidence that activity and good physical health leads to improved mental health and vice versa (Business in the Community, 2009). Research has shown that effective workplace mental health promotion programmes can produce a return on investment of £9 for every £1 invested (Knapp et al, 2011).

However, even if most employees are healthy, positive and productive most of the time, there will always be individual life events or vulnerabilities that can cause severe and long-lasting distress.

For a person in distress, in addition to unshakeable low mood or anxiety, there is embarrassment, fear of being thought weak or a poor bet for promotion and all the stigma still associated with mental illness. For colleagues and managers there is the worry that a key person is not performing, a hesitation or embarrassment about asking what is wrong for fear of intruding on private grief, or the worry that if the person does say what is wrong they will not know what to say. If the person even hints at feelings that involve self-harm or even suicide, there comes the additional worry that you might say the wrong thing and make matters worse.

All too often these factors cause the employee to try to hide their distress and clam up – maybe until things get so bad they cannot face going to work at all. For everyone else there is a strong impulse to keep their distance from the distressed individual and desperately hope that someone else will know what to do. These are entirely understandable reactions, but for the individual experiencing mental ill-health they are harder to recover from than the symptoms of the illness and can lead to career death and ruined lives. What a person in distress most needs is a supportive social environment and help with both the triggers and the manifestations of their condition. Treatment for depression and anxiety is effective, but in the UK 75% of people with these conditions get no professional help (McManus *et al*, 2009).

Employers can begin by acknowledging that depression and anxiety are common conditions and by encouraging staff to seek help when they become unwell. Line managers are crucial. Yet the majority of managers in the UK lack confidence and don't know what to do (Employers' Forum on Disability, 2008). There is thus a clear need for managers to develop the knowledge, skills and confidence to respond wisely and positively to mental health conditions.

Workplace training is one means of building this capability in line managers, as part of a business-wide commitment to supporting mental health at work. An evaluation of the Centre for Mental Health's workplace training, for example, found that participants became more confident about identifying and supporting employees with depression and anxiety, both immediately after the training and, more importantly, eight months later. They were more willing to talk to a person with depression, and some two-fifths had already made use of the training in a real life situation within eight months (Lockett & Grove, 2010).

Among the most difficult areas for managers is knowing what sources of help to suggest and what discretion they actually have to make temporary adjustments to workload etc. Larger companies increasingly have 'employee assistance programmes' or counselling providers to whom they can point people, as well as policies that support a certain amount of managerial discretion. For smaller companies, it may be that encouragement to see the GP or look at reputable self-help resources is the best that can be offered, but the important thing is that the message will have been given that the distressed individual is a valued member of staff and can expect concern and consideration rather than ignoring or scapegoating.

Rehabilitation and return to work

For most people, professional help combined with workplace support and adjustments for a short period will be sufficient to help them to recover. For those not recovering as expected, longer and more intensive treatment may be required. The government's new Health and Work Service will aim to offer treatment and support to people who have been off work for four weeks or more. The Department for Work and Pensions website describes the role of the service and the tax exemption for treatments recommended by it:

'There are two elements to the service:

- *assessment – once the employee has reached, or is expected to reach, 4 weeks of sickness absence they will normally be referred by their GP for an assessment by an occupational health professional, who will look at all the issues preventing the employee from returning to work*

- *advice – employers, employees and GPs will be able to access advice through a phone line and website*

Following an assessment, employees will receive a return to work plan with recommendations to help them to return to work more quickly and information on how to get appropriate help and advice.

We will introduce a tax exemption of up to £500 a year for each employee on medical treatments recommended by the Health and Work Service or an employer-arranged occupational health service.'

(For more information, see: https://www.gov.uk/government/policies/helping-people-to-find-and-stay-in-work/supporting-pages/co-ordinating-the-health-work-and-wellbeing-initiative)

As well as ensuring that people receive appropriate treatment and support for their health condition, keeping workplace relationships intact while treatment takes effect in many cases produces surprisingly good outcomes, enhancing employee loyalty, reducing tribunals and preventing the ruination of life chances.

For the employer, the important factors for someone who is on long-term sick leave are:

- To remain in touch. Continuing contact with the manager and the company should be enshrined in company policy, with managers trained in what to say to maintain hope and to give an expectation of return without verging on harassment.

- To create a return to work plan. There is increasing evidence that case management, in which people are given joined-up support to help them back to work and manage their condition (Seymour, 2010), is helpful when an employee is too low to make important, possibly life-changing decisions unaided, or if they feel unable to advocate for themselves.

Although acute symptoms need to be mostly under control for people to feel able to resume work, full symptomatic recovery is not necessary. Indeed, going back to work may be 'just what the doctor ordered', as long as it is carefully planned and involves all the key people.

Any workplace adjustments must address the problems likely to be encountered directly and be reasonable and affordable (which the evidence suggests most are). Most important of all is agreeing what should be said to whom. Mental illness is still heavily stigmatised by some people. Anticipated discrimination can be as important and damaging as actual discrimination (Thornicroft, 2006) so it is important that the returning employee feels in control of what colleagues and others know about them.

The government's Access to Work programme funds workplace adjustments for disabled people. At present, just three per cent of Access to Work funding is used to support people with mental health conditions in work, yet there is growing evidence of the benefits this can bring, providing both employer and employee with the reassurance that they need.

Support into employment

The employment rate of people with severe and enduring mental health problems is the lowest of all disability groups, at less than 10%, and yet the research evidence on what works in supported employment for this group is particularly strong (Centre for Mental Health, 2013). Research shows that the most effective method of supported employment for people with severe and enduring mental health problems is Individual Placement and Support (IPS).

IPS was developed in the US in the 1990s and has been replicated and successfully demonstrated in many other places including the UK, Norway, Denmark, Hong Kong, Canada, New Zealand and Australia. A six-centre randomised control trial (Burns *et al*, 2007) found that IPS was around twice as effective as the best alternative vocational rehabilitation service at achieving paid work outcomes in all sites, and also noted that people entering work did so more quickly and sustained their employment for longer in the IPS services than the alternatives.

To be effective, supported employment services have to work faithfully to the eight principles of IPS:

1. Competitive employment is the primary goal.
2. Everyone who wants it is eligible for employment support.
3. Job search is in line with individual preferences and strengths.
4. Job search is rapid – it begins within four weeks.
5. Employment specialist and clinical teams work and are located together.
6. Support is time-unlimited and individualised to both the employee and the employer.
7. Welfare benefits advice and information is available.
8. Jobs are developed with local employers.

The spread of IPS is still patchy, but more and more mental health services now offer it. The Centre for Mental Health has recognised 13 sites as IPS 'centres of excellence', where fidelity to the evidence-based model, including excellent employer engagement strategies and effective partnership working between employment support workers and health professionals, are evident. However, even in most of those high-performing areas not all the clinical teams have an assigned IPS worker, and therefore there are still large numbers of people who are denied access to an IPS service. We know what is needed, we just need to see it implemented everywhere, so that having access to IPS services is not dependent on being lucky enough to live in the right area.

The evidence base for IPS is predicated on trials within secondary care settings. There are, however, promising examples of the success of using the IPS model with primary care mental health teams. There are IPS workers in some IAPT (Improving Access to Psychological Therapies) services, including Wolverhampton Healthy Minds and Wellbeing Service. Extending and adapting IPS to primary care for people with common mental health problems was among the major recommendations of a government-commissioned report by RAND Europe (van Stolk *et al*, 2014) which is, at the time of writing, being piloted in four areas of England.

There is also evidence that IPS can be successfully adapted to people with drug or alcohol addictions (Centre for Mental Health, 2014) and a pilot to support people with mental health problems leaving prison into employment is also currently under way.

Conclusion

Businesses both large and small are now more aware than ever of mental health at work. But few know what to do about it and myths and misperceptions continue to cloud the issue. This fear and ignorance carries a heavy cost that a few simple steps can help to avoid. Recognising that mental ill-health is a normal part of life, and being prepared to be open and honest about it, is a first step any organisation can take. Making the change is as good for the health of a business as it is for the health of its staff.

For too many people, however, having a mental health condition means losing work or being told you may never work because of your illness. Attitudes are beginning to change in this regard, too, but the provision of effective support for people with a range of mental health problems to stay in work or get a new job is patchy. We need to see concerted action from government, health services, local authorities and employment services to offer support that works for people with mental health problems who want to work.

More information

More information about managing mental health at work and on supporting people with mental health problems into employment is available at www.centreformentalhealth.org.uk

References

Burns T, Catty J, Becker T, Drake R, Fioritti A & Knapp M (2007) The effectiveness of supported employment for people with severe mental illness: a randomized controlled trial in six European countries. *The Lancet* **370** 1146–1152.

Business in the Community (2009) *Emotional Resilience Toolkit* [online]. Available at: http://www.bitc. org.uk/our-resources/report/emotional-resilience (accessed January 2015).

Centre for Mental Health (2013) *Barriers to Employment: What works for people with mental health problems*. London: Centre for Mental Health.

Centre for Mental Health (2014) *Employment Support and Addiction: What works*. London: Centre for Mental Health.

Employers' Forum on Disability (2008) *Government's Mental Health Plans Must Include Line Managers*. London: Business Disability Forum.

Knapp M, McDaid D & Parsonage M (2011) *Mental Health Promotion and Mental Illness Prevention: The economic case*. London: Department of Health.

Lockett H & Grove B (2010) Responding to mental distress at work: Part 2: does workplace mental health training have a lasting impact? *Occupational Health at Work* **7** 20–23.

McManus S, Meltzer H, Brugha T, Bebbington P & Jenkins R (2009) *Adult Psychiatric Morbidity in England: Results of a household survey*. London: NHS Information Centre.

Sainsbury Centre (2007) *Mental Health at Work*. London: Centre for Mental Health.

Seymour L (2010) *Common Mental Health Problems at Work*. London: Centre for Mental Health and British Occupational Health Research Foundation.

Thornicroft G (2006) *Shunned: Discrimination against people with mental illness*. Oxford: Oxford University Press.

van Stolk C, Hofman J, Hafner M & Janta B (2014) *Psychological Wellbeing and Work: Improving service provision and outcomes*. London: Department for Work and Pensions and Department of Health.

Waddell G & Burton A (2006) *Is Work Good for Your Health and Wellbeing?* Norwich: The Stationery Office.

Chapter 8: A crisis of meaning? Searching for an antidote to the pathological picturing of distress

By Naomi James

Introduction

The theme of this chapter is the problem of seeing, hearing and representing lives within 'unstable' systems of care. Many who are embroiled in the mental health system, critical of psychiatry's medicalising approach as 'subjugating and impersonal', continue to identify a 'crisis of meaning' (Rogers & Pilgrim, 2005).

As radical economic reform of both mental health care and welfare provision is taking place, pathological labelling increasingly dominates in mental health spaces. People's own sense of meaning, identity, belonging and narrative can become silenced, disrupted and overwritten by the dominant medical discourse. From this critical perspective, a person's narrative, reduced to a label and seen through the lens of the medical model, renders invisible the realities of social lives and associated distress. Distress is a major organising factor in the way stories about our mental health are told.

This chapter will speak to those of you interested in working within an alternative model that draws from narrative psychology, a field of research and practice focused on the way stories shape lives. Participatory video will be explored as one creative practice that can help develop sensitive methodologies to meaningfully involve and access the worlds of people with experience of distress.

The chapter will emphasise how Mike White and David Epston's concept of 're-authoring' (White & Epston, 1990), originating in narrative psychology, can be usefully applied to participatory video – an emergent research practice that can express difference in a new way and give meaning to those expressions of experience, which could otherwise be discarded as incoherent or marginal.

Conceived as a process that places control of representation in the hands of the represented, participatory video offers an inclusive way to investigate emotional health and gives credence to 'service user' and/or 'survivor' controlled research.

The aims of this chapter are to explore both the potential for, and limitations of, creative action-research methodologies to create the conditions for people who experience distress to:

- play an equal role in mental health practice and research as experts in their own lives

- contribute to other ways of seeing and give meaning to emotional disturbances

- take up their personal power in presenting and examining what it means to be emotionally healthy

- directly influence and share in the power and process of knowledge production.

It will ask what the potential is of this emergent action-research process to re-qualify local knowledge and bring counter-cultural descriptions of mental health and distress to the fore. In what ways can it provide an antidote to unjust practices of power, and how can it remedy the neglect of the biographical and social?

A conflicting system

The introduction of the Health and Social Care Act (2012), promising more choice, shared decision-making, power and control, has seen the continued rise in rates of de facto and compulsory detention. The Care Quality Commission reported that restraint was being used on a daily basis, over a quarter (27%) of care plans showed no involvement of the person they were written for and 22% showed no sign of a person's view nor values being taken into account (2014). From the perspective of a person who accesses services, that is 'many decisions about me, taken without me'.

Multiple and conflicting versions of mental health and recovery are enacted through mental health policy and practice, underpinned by research predicated on a dominant medical model of understanding mental health. Such understandings privilege pharmacological interventions over the biographical and are propagated by the current system and its policies. This approach tends to diminish personal agency, discourage diversity, silence voices and is shaped by global norms promoting an individualist 'encapsulated self' (White, 2005).

In the West, stories of adversity often emphasise the individual in society and focus on normative conceptions and interpretations of the stories people tell of their lives. Making sense of people's life experience is often approached as a neat, linear and orderly project; however when this is translated into practice and applied to real lived experience, there is a lot of slippage.

Arthur Kleinman warns that chronicity (having an illness of long duration) arises in part in the telling of dead or static stories:

> '...situating the individual in a wasteland, a denervated place, robbed of its fertility and potential. Possessing and perpetuating a narrative of 'incurability' may serve many protective and defensive purposes for psychiatric staff involved and even offer some comfort and orientation to a vulnerable or dependent individual; but in doing so we may collude with building walls and tearing down bridges.'

(Kleinman, 1988, p180)

Power is one of the central shaping forces for understanding how people situate themselves, show, express and share stories of their lives. If we take 'to empower' to mean 'to enable, to permit, to give', then the real power rests with those in authority. In this context, the term 'empowerment' in mental health has become inverted. From a critical stance I ask: where is the power in empowerment? How can people reclaim power for themselves?

The need for the development of creative methodologies

Within the 'survivor'/'service user' movement, there is disillusionment with existing involvement practices and research paradigms, resulting in a call for methodologies that are more relevant and meaningful to our lives. Most often it is people who communicate differently who are excluded from the research context. This can relate to barriers of language, ethnicity, impairment, people who do not communicate verbally and people who find it impossible to verbalise what has happened to them.

Sanderson and Kindon (2004) assert that, 'conventional social science relies on a process of external experts "extracting" information from passive subjects'.

The Disabled People's Movement has highlighted the importance of contesting and changing the social relations of research production (Beresford, 2002). The contention here is that service users/survivors remain much more liable to become the researched rather than researchers.

In *The Ethics of Survivor Research*, Faulkner presses on the reader the importance of research in generating creative alternatives, leading to change and not to knowledge for its own sake. She establishes, 'a vital component of the potential for research to facilitate empowerment lies in its commitment to change' (Faulkner, 2004).

Drawing from narrative psychology

The recovery movement has tended in recent years to valorise notions of self-possession, self-containment, self-reliance and self-sufficiency. A renewed vision of empowerment is needed, one that recognises our collective strengths and potential for the 'service user' community/'survivor' movement to claim back power and to continue to look together at how discursive structures both enable and limit the 'conditions of possibility' (Foucault, 1988) for the lived experience.

This may provide a response to Rappaport's (1993, 1995) call for a 'community narrative of empowerment' and represents a resistance to a purely 'self-help' model originating in an individualist ideology and a move towards collectivism. Rappaport envisaged that this approach could give 'psychiatric consumers'/'service users' a supportive context in which to 'reconstruct personal stories that re-enact emotional health, strengths, recovery and hope' (Rappaport, 1995, p795).

Narrative psychology, a field of research and practice that focuses on the way stories shape lives, provides a way that people with lived experience of distress can find meaning in their experience and strengthen their voices. Rather than being derived from structuralist psychological disciplines that conceive of permanent structures such as human nature and the unconscious, narrative psychology focuses on the social construction of selves and considers the processes of being – the how and not the what.

The concept of 'narrative re-authoring', developed by Mike White (2007), draws from Jacques Derrida's (Derrida & Bass, 1982) notion of 'deconstruction', whereby externalising the dominant problem-saturated stories of a person's life allows them to be listened to in order to identify spaces, gaps, alternative meanings or conflicting stories. White refers to this as a process of 'externalising, internalised discourse'. The influence that problems have in a person's life can be explored and mapped.

By adopting and developing concepts originating in narrative psychology that claim to enable individuals to separate their lives and narratives from those ideas and dominant discourses that they judge to be impoverishing, we might collaborate in new, creative methods of challenging the ways of life that people find subjugating. We can do this by encouraging them to re-visualise and re-author stories of their own lives according to alternative meanings and preferred stories of identity.

However, Crossley (2000) argues that it is not just the fact that people tell stories in making sense of themselves and others. She states that a narrative psychological approach:

'...goes far deeper than that. For, central to this approach, is the development of a phenomenological understanding of the unique "order of meaning". One of the main features of this "order of meaning" is the experience of time and temporality ... Everything experienced by human beings is made meaningful, understood and interpreted in relation to the primary dimension of "activity" which incorporates both "time" and "sequence".' (Crossley, 2000 p6)

Utilising time-based media as a way to support people to work with stories of their lives ensures the exploration of meaning in time, space and sequence which does not break the inextricable connections between the context of expression, temporality and identity. This has particular importance for mental health research, where experiences aren't so easily translated into words and coherent structured stories. The way we experience time during distress or a breakdown is often difficult to understand. Visual media provides a way to amass a range of expressions, memories and impressions of an experience to work them into a coherent whole that is not constrained by a purely linear, predestined or teleogenic plot.

Narrative psychology applied to participatory video

In her article 'Collaborative film-making as process, method and text in mental health research', Hester Parr (2007) explores the utilisation of filmmaking as a fieldwork art, arguing that it enables a range of processes and outcomes for vulnerable people – namely participative, social, technological and self-representational possibilities. Parr situates these as emergent strategies provided for researchers so that they might transcend traditional boundaries between 'expert researcher' and 'researched community'.

However, there is a common anxiety in mental health research over the ethics of identifying participants, which is usually overcome by anonymising them. Research has often silenced and 'colluded with building walls' (Kleinman, 1988) in the name of protecting people from their own stories and expressions of their lives. Conversely, the use of creative methodologies like participatory video are a less passive and more inclusive and active process, one that does not emphasise and reinforce shame and stigma by instilling the idea that problems are private and therefore hidden and often silent. The method can instead be public, political and capable of bringing about real change.

Rooted in the struggle of generations to strengthen their voice, the National Survivor User Network has developed a robust framework for valuing experience in the context of involvement. The National Involvement Standards (Faulkner, 2015), referred to as 4PI, consist of: Principles, Purpose, Presence, Process and Impact. This framework provides a useful structure to ensure the practical application of participatory video stays true to our values and can bring about real change.

In planning any participatory video project it will be helpful to reference and apply these standards.

Principles

Through all phases of the participatory video method there must be a commitment to:

- **openness, trust, equality and respect:** authenticity of expression will only be captured in video if a safe space is created and maintained

- **sharing and exploring values, beliefs, emotions and actions:** adequate time must be given to ensure people's stories are honoured and are authored by the people rather than those facilitating

- **an ethical framework in place at all times:** to ensure a strong feeling of personal safety, informed consent must be regularly revisited and the video data must be securely stored. Participants must be able to opt out at any stage

- **sensitivity to language and expression:** participants will need to develop a shared way to name and therefore define video clips reflecting their experiences

- **recognising and minimising power differentials:** the use of the video camera in participatory video does not usually involve fixed camera positions, suggestive of surveillance. Participants are encouraged to handle the camera and make its position fluid and changing, thus avoiding a 'panoptical lens'

- **people taking part are given the technical support they need to realise the vision of their story:** technical abilities must not be a barrier to a person having full authorship of their story.

Purpose

The core purpose of using participatory video in mental health must be to strengthen participant's voices and ultimately improve lives. This will involve:

- **agreement** on the reasons and motivations for using video to visualise life experiences
- **recognition** that this may mean people stepping out of their comfort zone
- **speaking** out to challenge stigma and discrimination
- **checking** people's understanding of re-authoring their experiences.

Presence

The presence of people from a variety of cultures ensures that the experiences shared and stories told are rich, meaningful and considered from a variety of perspectives. The role of all people taking part must be to:

- **share**, witness, capture, respond and re-author important experiences and stories of life
- **step** away from common responses of making value judgements
- **reflect** on how people's life experience has impact on them
- **listen** for gaps and contradictions in people's stories of experience allowing alternative, subordinate meanings to emerge
- **allow** people the space and opportunity to break free from the constraints of a deterministic plot
- **create** a space for people to see their life experiences in different ways
- **let** the camera mediate more than just verbal dialogue.

Process

The process of participatory video is agreed with all participants from the start, as equal partners. It can follow a four-phase structure of a 'definitional ceremony' (White, 2007) where people who are witness to the story are crucial also to the re-authoring of the stories. People in a group can form a story circle for:

- **telling** – testimony recorded in video

- **retelling** – a screening of the testimony, listening for subordinate plotlines and looking out for neglected but significant events in the video that seem out of phase with the dominant storyline. Elements are explored such as rhythm, intensity, connection, disconnection, protesting, reaching out, protection, gesture, turning points, movement and space. Group analysis of the stories using a coding or 'memo-ing' process to define and name clips of the video story

- **re-authoring** – editing and re-editing the video story based on learning from the retelling

- **community response** – deciding to share with a wider audience, a screening for people to collectively witness the re-authored story.

Impact

If the participatory video methodology is to be meaningful then it is about bringing change in cycles of improvement through:

- **capturing**, strengthening and sharing voices

- **finding** meaning and a main message

- **intensifying** the message

- **feeling** heard

- **being** seen

- **exploring** the extent to which those taking part think it provides an antidote to pathological pictures of distress

- **acknowledging** video as a text that holds and visualises changes and transformation

- **attending** closely to the full repertoire of our meaning making processes

- **showing** how the different axes of identity interact to produce human lived experience

- **challenging** the status quo of knowledge production

- **reflecting** continually on the method and practice – there is a need to keep raising the debate about meaning and representation (by whom and about whom).

Over the years of practising it, I have witnessed the power of participatory video to promote a sense of ownership and belonging among people who may have previously positioned themselves at the margins. I conceive of the camera as a space of mobilisation and of mediation rather than simply a methodological tool.

The work of curating selves using participatory video offers the ability to visualise transformational shifts in people's lives by contributing to a wider cultural change in ways other methods do not.

Warning against misapplication: the tyranny of participatory video

Participatory methods can serve to bolster and maintain existing power relationships, and the process of participatory video research can be reasonably equated with power, but empowerment may not consequentially follow.

Participation itself is in danger of becoming a commodity that groups and organisations use to advance their corporate image. It can even be used by governments to advance a false sense of community cohesion, for example by making people happy in poverty. We must remind ourselves regularly of the purpose of the approach – first and foremost to strengthen the direct voice of people. Paul Francis (2001) argues in *Participation: The new tyranny?* that 'participatory approaches characterised by concern for sustainability, relevance and empowerment can still be an abuse of power'. He warns of, 'a kind of ventriloquism (that) sees the expression of dominant interests as community concerns, external interests as internal need' (Francis, 2001 p5).

The task of developing this method is to consistently honour ways in which subjectivity and agency in mental health can be dynamically enacted and experienced. Imaging technology reveals innovative possibilities for transformational activism and for shaping individual and community development. It is crucial to pay close attention to ensure projects are realistic and are steered from the ground up, serving to represent the emerging concerns of the participants rather than preconceived outsider agendas.

Conclusion

'We create ourselves out of the stories we tell about our lives, stories that impose purpose and meaning on experiences that often seem random and discontinuous. As we scrutinize our past in the effort to explain ourselves to ourselves we discover or invent consistent motivations, characteristic patterns, values, a sense of self. Fashioned out of our memories, our stories become our identities.'

(Faust, 2003, p205)

Participatory video, drawing from narrative psychology, provides an exciting and significant framework and methodology for meaningful involvement, to investigate the personal as a community issue and reimagine people in society. 'Re-authoring' can be a useful concept for 'service user' and 'survivor' researchers to take up their personal power and author their own stories of their lives. People can positively use tools like participatory video to capture and spread the plurality of voices and harness them as a catalyst for change.

The focus of the methodology is not the transformation of selves, our identities into new subjects, but lies in the particular form of the remembered moment, making visible the constitutive powers of the subject-in-process. It must focus on the process by which selves are understood, to make visible the modes of subjection.

This position echoes Foucault (1988) who sees the work of self-transformation as 'freeing oneself from one's self'. From this perspective, selves are constituted through and with other people and are not static but evolve historically. People in transformation are determined by the subjective processes of the era. The projection of self, Foucault argues, is altered by actively resisting the dominant processes of subjection within our era.

'We are not only what we do in a world of images; we are also what we show ourselves to be. It is a crucial medium of resistance and counter-discourse.' (Renov, 2004)

References

Beresford P (2002) User involvement in research and evaluation: liberation or regulation? *Social Policy and Society* **1** (2) 95–105.

Care Quality Commission (2014) *Monitoring the Mental Health Act in 2012/13* [online]. Available at: http://www.cqc.org.uk/sites/default/files/documents/cqc_mentalhealth_2012_13_07_update.pdf (accessed February 2015).

Crossely M (2000) *Introducing Narrative Psychology: Self, trauma and the construction of meaning*. Buckingham: Open University Press.

Derrida J & Bass A (1982) *Positions*. Chicago: University of Chicago Press.

Faulkner A (2004) *The Ethics of Survivor Research: Guidelines for the ethical conduct of research carried out by mental health service users and survivors*. Bristol: Policy Press.

Faulkner A (2015) *National Involvement Partnership 4PI Standards for Involvement* [online]. London: NSUN. Available at: www.nsun.org.uk/about-us/our-work/national-involvement-partnership (accessed March 2015).

Faust DG (2003) Living history [online]. *Harvard Magazine* **May–June**. Available at: http://harvardmagazine.com/2003/05/living-history.html (accessed February 2015).

Foucault M (1988) *Technologies of the Self: A seminar with Michel Foucault*. Amherst, MA: University of Massachusetts Press.

Francis P (2001) Participatory development at the World Bank: the primacy of process. In: B Cooke and U Kothari (Eds) *Participation: The New Tyranny?* New York: Zed Books.

Kleinman A (1988) *The Illness Narratives: Suffering, healing, and the human condition.* New York: Basic Books.

Parr H (2007) Collaborative film-making as process, method and text in mental health research. *Cultural Geographies* **14** (1) 114–138.

Rappaport J (1993) Narrative studies, personal stories, and identity transformation in the mutual help context. *Journal of Applied Behavioral Science* **29** (2) 239–256.

Rappaport J (1995) Empowerment meets narrative: listening to stories and creating settings. *American Journal of Community Psychology* **23** (5) 795–807.

Renov M (2004) *The Subject of Documentary.* Minneapolis: University of Minnesota Press.

Rogers A & Pilgrim D (2005) *A Sociology of Mental Health and Illness.* Maidenhead: Open University Press.

Sanderson E & Kindon, S (2004) Progress in participatory development: opening up the possibility of knowledge through progressive participation. *Progress in Development Studies* **4** (2) 114–126.

White M (2005) *Workshop Notes* [online]. Dulwich Centre. Available at: www.dulwichcentre.com.au/michael-white-workshop-notes.pdf (accessed March 2015).

White M (2007) *Maps of Narrative Practice.* London: Norton Professional Books.

White M & Epston D (1990) *Narrative Means to Therapeutic Ends.* New York: WW Norton.

Chapter 9: Is old age a mental illness?

By Toby Williamson

Introduction

The theme of World Mental Health Day in 2013 was older adults, that of 2012 was depression, and 2014's was schizophrenia. Given that the term 'mental health' is commonly (mis)used or (mis)interpreted as referring to mental illness, together with negative connotations associated with health and old age, later life may well seem to be synonymous with mental health problems.

Although defining the parameters of later life can be difficult, we do know that the populations of most European countries and North America are ageing – more people are growing older, and older people are living longer. The UK is no exception (see Box 9.1). Longevity should be a cause for celebration and the majority of people have mentally healthy later lives and continue to contribute in many different ways to society. Yet society often appears ambivalent in its views about older people, ignoring, criticising or demeaning them, and for many older people later life can be a time of poor mental health and significant cognitive decline. This chapter explores key aspects, and challenges assumptions about, mental health in later life.

What is ageing?

Although we talk about the UK and other countries having ageing societies, defining 'later life' or 'old age' is far from straightforward. Definitions of age range from 'chronological' age (ie. the number of years we have lived since birth), through 'biological' age (wear and tear on the body occurs at different rates for different people depending on a variety of factors), to 'psychological' and 'social' age (one is 'as old as one feels' or how old society perceives you to be).

There are several different theories of ageing, ranging from moving through pre-ordained stages of life (epitomised by William Shakespeare's poem, *The Seven Stages of Man*) to much more dynamic theories that recognise the effect that life events, social, economic and other factors in society, and the ability of the individual to effect change in themselves, have on a person as they grow old. A concise summary of definitions of age and theories of ageing is contained in McCulloch (2009).

However, for the purposes of this chapter, the age of 50 is being used as a rough benchmark for the start of later life. I hear a sharp intake of breath and the beginnings of protest: 'I'm 55 and I'm not old!' That's fair enough, and respecting self-definitions of age is important as well as acknowledging that chronological age is not everything. But people in their 50s may be paying increasing attention to retiring from paid work, if they have children these are usually grown up and may have moved away, and events linked with later life are becoming more commonplace – loss and bereavement, physical changes and the onset of health conditions associated with old age (with resulting increases in care dependencies).

Yet it is important to note that increasing numbers of people in their 50s also have parents still alive, so one might also argue that there are two generations of older people. There are those people born pre-World War II who are in their mid-70s or older, and the so-called 'baby boomers' born immediately after the war (and in a second wave in the late 1950s and early 1960s) who are in their 50s and mid-60s (Mental Health Foundation, 2013). Growing up in wartime Britain was a very different experience from growing up during the 1960s, so there are very significant differences in the life course and life experience of these two groups (although there are also considerable variations within generations) and this, together with the differences in their chronological age, is of considerable significance in relation to their mental health and experience of mental health problems. This clearly exposes the problem of talking about people in later life as if they were a homogenous whole, and it is also important in how it informs attitudes and policy concerning mental health in later life.

Despite the changing demographics of our society, later life is often viewed or portrayed in very negative terms, with a sense of being a 'burden on society', something to be feared, and consisting primarily of an unpleasant combination of health conditions and problems – dementia and depression to name but two (the language used in the media around dementia is particularly negative with terms such as 'living death' and 'silent plague' commonly employed). The 'baby boomer' generation have come in for particular criticism as having benefited from the post-war boom and then having either spent or squirrelled away their earnings in ways that subsequent generations couldn't benefit from, yet becoming dependent upon them as growing numbers require care and support for health problems they develop as they grow older. Making generalisations about such a large and complex cohort of the population inevitably paints an inaccurate picture and, as we shall see, negative representations of older people are a significant factor relating to mental health in later life.

Box 9.1: Ageing in the UK

- A third of the UK population (21 million people) is over the age of 50. Ten million are over 65.

- For the first time in UK history there are more people aged over 60 than under the age of 18.

- The fastest population increase has been in the number of people age 85 and over.

- One in five people alive in the UK today can expect to reach the age of 100. In 1986 there were around 2,600 centenarians – there are now over 12,000.

- Life expectancy continues to increase – a man aged 65 in 2013 could expect to live another 18.5 years (compared to 12 years in 1963) and 21 years for a woman (compared to 16 years in 1963). But healthy life expectancy (years lived without a disability or illness) is not keeping pace with overall life expectancy. The same man could expect to live 7½ of those years in ill health and the woman nine years. And these figures mask big socio-economic differences – a man born in central Glasgow can expect to live almost 14 years less than a man born in Kensington and Chelsea.

(Age UK, 2014)

Mental health in later life

All the evidence indicates that the majority of older people experience good mental health in later life. Mental health problems commonly associated with old age, such as depression and dementia, only affect a minority of people and are therefore not inevitable aspects of growing old. For example, the Office of National Statistics survey on personal well-being found that people aged between 65–79 reported the highest levels of any age group for feeling that the things they do in life are worthwhile and bring a sense of happiness (Office of National Statistics, 2013).

But good mental health in later life is not entirely due to the luck of the draw. Five key factors are particularly important in relation to mental health in later life:

- an adequate income

- being treated with respect as an older person and not being discriminated against or viewed negatively on the basis of age

- reasonably good physical health

■ positive social relationships

■ opportunities for meaningful activity and participation in community and society.

(Mental Health Foundation & Age Concern, 2006)

While most of these apply to people of all ages, later life gives them a particular 'spin'. Income can change significantly as a result of retirement or needing social care (which is not universally free in most parts of the UK in the way that healthcare is). Physical health, mobility, vision and hearing can all deteriorate dramatically with age, relationships and friendships often decrease as a result of bereavements, and participation in meaningful activities may also decline as a result of retirement, poor health or technological exclusion. Sixty per cent of older people in the UK believe that age discrimination exists in the daily lives of older people (Age UK, 2014) and the negative portrayals and common stereotypes of older people are evidence of ageism. (For more information on looking after one's mental health in later life, see Mental Health Foundation, 2011.)

Chronological age, other aspects of demography (eg. ethnicity), and socio-economic factors together with lifestyle and psychological factors (eg. coping ability), mean that the older people's experience of these factors and their impact vary greatly. However, they certainly point to the importance of transitions (eg. retirement, loss of a loved one, onset of illness and changes in care dependency) as being potentially crucial in a person's mental health, as well as the fact that many older people may have experienced mental health problems earlier in life which are ongoing issues or may reoccur at some point.

Box 9.2 summarises the most common mental health problems and conditions in later life. It should be noted, however, that under-reporting and low rates of diagnosis of mental health problems and conditions is a particular feature of later life. Older people have tended to be more reluctant to acknowledge experiencing difficulties with their mental health or seek help, and there is evidence to indicate this is particularly the case with certain groups, such as older men and some ethnic minorities (Williamson, 2010). Furthermore, some doctors have been reluctant to diagnose because they have viewed problems such as depression to be an inevitable part of ageing and, in the case of dementia, because effective treatments and support are lacking ('therapeutic nihilism'). As a result, diagnosis rates for conditions such as dementia are as low as 40% (of known prevalence) in some parts of the UK (Alzheimer's Society, 2014). Older people are also much more likely to have two or more health problems or conditions (comorbidities): most people over the age of 65 have two or more long-term health conditions and most people over 75 have three (Barnett *et al*, 2012).

Box 9.2: Mental health problems and conditions in later life

- Between six and 13% of people aged over 65 say they feel always or very lonely.

- Depression affects 22% of men and 28% of women aged over 65 (around two million people) compared to 8–12% of the population overall. It is estimated that 85% of them receive no help from the NHS.

- 800,000 people in the UK have some form of dementia. The most common form is Alzheimer's disease (62% of people with dementia). Two-thirds of people with dementia live in their own homes.

- The risk of developing dementia increases with age: it affects one in 14 people aged over 65 but one in six people aged over 80. The number of people with dementia in the UK is estimated to be over a million by 2021.

- It is estimated that up to 50% of people with dementia also have depression.

- There are no cures or long-lasting, universally effective treatments for any form of dementia.

- It is estimated that dementia costs the UK approximately £23 billion per year – twice as much as cancer – yet the UK spends nearly 12 times as much on cancer research than it does on dementia research.

- Other problems that are increasingly prevalent in later life (mainly for demographic reasons) include anxiety, delirium, psychotic conditions and harmful use of alcohol and drugs.

(Age UK, 2007; Victor, 2011; Gottfries, 2001)

Mental health services in later life

Until very recently, older people's mental health was treated separately from that of adults of 'working age'. Separate mental health services were provided for older people based on the argument that there were very significant differences in the manifestation and experience of mental health problems in later life which required specialist expertise and interventions. Certainly, the fact that dementia is largely a mental health condition that appears in later life provided a strong justification for this approach. The government's Mental Health National Service Framework (NSF) for England, published in 1999 (Department of Health, 1999) only covered services for adults under the age of 65 and there was a separate NSF for older people that contained a section on mental health (Department of Health, 2001). Social care provided by local authorities for older people (although the age threshold varied) was also separate from care provided to younger adults and, for older adults with mental health problems or dementia, it tended to be dominated by more traditional services such as residential care.

Yet there were problems with this approach. It was argued that having an age threshold created artificial distinctions and barriers. Shouldn't services be designed around need rather than age? What was the difference between someone who developed depression at the age of 63 compared to someone else who developed it at the age of 66? Access to dementia services for people who developed dementia before the age of 65 was often problematic and even if they did receive a service these were often designed around the needs of much older people.[5] Older people's mental health services often had only limited expertise concerning older people diagnosed with psychosis, bipolar disorder or personality disorders as these are less common in later life. The separation was seen to reinforce ageism and the view that old age was a health problem in its own right. And, perhaps most significantly, while there was considerable investment made in adult mental health services as a result of the mental health NSF, no significant investment was forthcoming from the older people's NSF for later life mental health services (Mental Health Foundation, 2009).

Recent developments

Over the last 10 years, growing calls to challenge age discrimination and abolish the default retirement age in 2011 (meaning that employers could no longer require employees to retire at 65 and rendering the term 'working age adult' obsolete) signalled changes in wider society's approach to its ageing population. In 2010, the Equality Act made discrimination in the provision of goods and services based on age unlawful, although the ban only came into force in 2012. This meant that it became unlawful to provide different health and social care services for adults based purely on age. Specialist mental health services that hitherto had only been accessible to people under the age of 65 (eg. home treatment and crisis teams, and many psychological therapies) now had to be provided to older people as well, should they need them. Mental health policy for older people is now part of the government's overall mental health strategy, *No Health Without Mental Health* (Department of Health, 2011) and differences in social care services can no longer be justified on the basis of age.

How far mental health services have changed to become 'age inclusive' is still difficult to know. There has been resistance from some old age mental health services to being incorporated into general adult services, fearing that older people will not receive a service responsive to their needs (as well as possibly fearing for their own future). It is certainly the case that dementia requires a different approach from other mental health problems because it is an organic

---

5   There are at least 17,000 people with dementia below that age in the UK, and the figure may be much higher.

illness (unlike other mental health problems), and since 2009 there has been a separate government strategy for dementia (Department of Health, 2009), which has now been superseded by the *Prime Minister's Challenge on Dementia* (Department of Health, 2012a[6]). However, there is a concern that the focus on dementia has meant that other mental health services for older people may have been neglected; the 2011/12 *National Survey of Investment in Mental Health Services* (Department of Health, 2012b) showed that there was a one per cent decrease in overall investment in mental health services but a three per cent decrease for older people's mental health services.

Looking to the future

There is no indication that the increasing risk of being affected by mental health problems and dementia as one grows older is likely to be reversed or that an effective treatment for the most common forms of dementia will be found in the near future. Together with physical illnesses and conditions associated with old age, social and economic factors (such as people living longer with inadequate pensions) and negative perceptions of later life, mentally healthy ageing is still something that many are unable to achieve, although recently there has been an increased focus on preventative factors for dementia (Public Health England & UK Health Forum, 2014; Alzheimer's Disease International, 2014). Older people are also the biggest users of health and social care services, and as their numbers grow this places an increasing demand on publicly funded services at a time when those services are having their budgets cut or severely restricted as a result of the government's 'austerity' policy. It is still too early to say whether making services 'age inclusive' will benefit older people although recent figures from the Improved Access to Psychological Therapies programme (IAPT) show that only 6.5% of people using IAPT services were aged 64 and over (IAPT, 2014). Personalisation in health and social care may over time lead to a reduction in residential care (although this may be offset by growing numbers of very old, frail and highly dependent people) and appeal to many in the baby boomer population, but, to date, key elements of the policy such as personal budgets have been least popular with older people compared to other groups.

On the other hand, and not least because of sheer numbers, people can be reasonably optimistic about their mental health in later life. According to a study published on Older People's Day in 2013 by Global AgeWatch Index using a range of factors to measure quality of life, the UK is the 13th best country in the world to grow old in (higher than Spain and Italy – Sweden was top). There is some

---

6 An update on progress on the Prime Minister's Challenge was published in 2015 (Department of Health, 2015).

evidence to indicate that many in the baby boomer generation are 'reinventing' old age as a continuation of adulthood rather than a separate, final phase, and are more likely to seek help for mental health problems if they experience them (Mental Health Foundation, 2013). Older people have better legal protection to prevent discrimination based on age and may be better able to adapt to and utilise technology and other changes in society.

Perhaps somewhat surprisingly there is no significant evidence to indicate that having dementia or experiencing cognitive decline as one grows older is automatically associated with a decrease in quality of life or mental well-being (Woods, 2012). In other words, it is possible to adapt and 'live well' with dementia for many years, providing one has the appropriate support, and this ability to adapt may mitigate some of the negative aspects of living longer in poor health. Positive representations of people living with dementia in public awareness campaigns, greater numbers of people living with the condition speaking out about their experiences to influence change, and the concepts of 'dementia friendly' and 'age friendly' also signify positive developments (Public Health England, 2013; Joseph Rowntree Foundation, 2012, 2014; World Health Organization, 2007).

Conclusion

While diagnosing a 'severe case of old age' might generate more money for pharmaceutical companies if they are developing a drug that reverses the ageing process, later life is not a mental health condition. Growing old is not something so separate from the rest of adult life (perhaps negating the need for a chapter like this), a burden on society, or something to be feared. Yet there are identifiable factors that impact on older people's mental health in ways that are frequently different to younger people, and there are differences in the prevalence and nature of mental health problems in later life. However mental health services are designed, they must be able to respond with that awareness and knowledge. The famous French singer and actor Maurice Chevalier once said that 'old age isn't so bad when you consider the alternative' – later life can and should be a lot more than that.

References

Age UK (2007) *Improving Services and Support for Older People with Mental Health Problems*. London: Age Concern.

Age UK (2014) *Later Life in the United Kingdom Factsheet November 2014* [online]. London: Age UK. Available at: http://www.ageuk.org.uk/Documents/EN-GB/Factsheets/Later_Life_UK_factsheet. pdf?dtrk=true (accessed January 2015).

Alzheimer's Disease International (2014) *World Alzheimer Report 2014: Dementia and risk reduction* [online]. London: Alzheimer's Disease International. Available at: http://www.alz.co.uk/research/world-report-2014 (accessed January 2015).

Alzheimer's Society (2014) *Dementia 2014: Opportunity for change* [online]. London: Alzheimer's Society. Available at: http://www.alzheimers.org.uk/site/scripts/documents_info.php?documentID=2313 (accessed January 2015).

Barnett K, Mercer S, Norbury M, Watt G, Wyke S & Guthrie B (2012) Epidemiology of multimorbidity and implications for health care, research, and medical education: a cross-sectional study. *The Lancet* **380** (9836) 37–43.

Department of Health (1999) *National Service Framework: Mental health*. London: Department of Health.

Department of Health (2001) *National Service Framework: Older people*. London: Department of Health.

Department of Health (2009) *Living Well with Dementia: A national dementia strategy* [online]. London: Department of Health. Available at: https://www.gov.uk/government/publications/living-well-with-dementia-a-national-dementia-strategy (accessed January 2015).

Department of Health (2011) *No Health Without Mental Health: A cross-government outcomes strategy* [online]. London: Department of Health. Available at: https://www.gov.uk/government/publications/no-health-without-mental-health-a-cross-government-outcomes-strategy (accessed January 2015).

Department of Health (2012a) *Prime Minister's Challenge on Dementia* [online]. London: Department of Health. Available at: https://www.gov.uk/government/publications/prime-ministers-challenge-on-dementia (accessed January 2015).

Department of Health (2012b) *2011/12 National Survey of Investment in Adult Mental Health Services* [online]. London: Department of Health. Available at: https://www.gov.uk/government/publications/investment-in-mental-health-in-2011-to-2012-working-age-adults-and-older-adults (accessed January 2015).

Department of Health (2015) *Prime Minister's Challenge on Dementia 2020* [online]. London: Department of Health. Available at: https://www.gov.uk/government/publications/prime-ministers-challenge-on-dementia-2020 (accessed February 2015).

Global AgeWatch Index (2013) *Global AgeWatch Index 2013: Insight report, summary and methodology* [online]. Available at: http://www.helpage.org/global-agewatch/reports/global-agewatch-index-2013-insight-report-summary-and-methodology/ (accessed January 2015).

Gottfries CG (2001) Late life depression. *European Archives of Psychiatry and Clinical Neuroscience* **251** (2) 73–9.

IAPT (2014) *Older People* [online]. Available at: http://www.iapt.nhs.uk/equalities/older-people/ (accessed January 2015).

Joseph Rowntree Foundation (2012) *A Stronger Collective Voice for People with Dementia* [online]. York: Joseph Rowntree Foundation. Available at: http://www.jrf.org.uk/publications/stronger-collective-voice (accessed January 2015).

Joseph Rowntree Foundation (2014) *Dementia Without Walls* [online]. York: Joseph Rowntree Foundation. Available at: http://www.jrf.org.uk/topic/dementia-without-walls (accessed January 2015).

McCulloch A (2009) Old age and mental health in the context of the life span: what are the key issues in the 21st century. In: T Williamson (Ed) *Older People's Mental Health Today: A handbook*. Brighton: Pavilion Publishing and Media.

Mental Health Foundation & Age Concern (2006) *Promoting Mental Health and Well-being in Later Life* [online]. London: Mental Health Foundation. Available at: http://www.mentalhealth.org.uk/publications/promoting-mental-health-and-well-being-in-later-life/ (accessed January 2015).

Mental Health Foundation (2009) *All Things Being Equal* [online]. London: Mental Health Foundation. Available at: http://www.mentalhealth.org.uk/publications/all-things-being-equal/ (accessed January 2015).

Mental Health Foundation (2011) *How to Look After Your Mental Health in Later Life*. London: Mental Health Foundation. Available at: http://www.mentalhealth.org.uk/publications/how-to-in-later-life (accessed January 2015).

Mental Health Foundation (2013) *Getting On… With Life. Baby boomers, mental health and ageing well* [online]. London: Mental Health Foundation. Available at: http://www.mentalhealth.org.uk/publications/getting-on-full-report/ (accessed January 2015).

Office of National Statistics (2013) *Statistical Bulletin: Personal well-being in the UK, 2012/13*. London: Office of National Statistics.

Public Health England (2013) *Dementia Friends Awareness Campaign* [film] [online]. Available at: https://www.youtube.com/watch?v=LfrnWrpPq54 (accessed January 2015).

Public Health England and UK Health Forum (2014) *Blackfriars Consensus on Promoting Brain Health: Reducing risk factors for dementia in the population*. London: Public Health England and UK Health Forum. Available at: http://nhfshare.heartforum.org.uk/RMAssets/Reports/Blackfriars%20 consensus%20%20_V18.pdf (accessed January 2015).

Victor C (2011) *Safeguarding the Convoy: A call to action from the Campaign to End Loneliness* [online]. Oxford: Age UK Oxfordshire. Available at: http://www.campaigntoendloneliness.org/wp-content/uploads/downloads/2011/07/safeguarding-the-convey_-_a-call-to-action-from-the-campaign-to-end-loneliness.pdf (accessed January 2015).

Williamson T (2010) Grumpy Old Men? Older men's mental health and emotional well-being. In: D Conrad and A White (Eds) *Promoting Men's Mental Health*. Abingdon: Radcliffe Publishing.

Woods B (2012) Well-being and dementia: how can it be achieved? *Quality in Ageing and Older Adults* **13** (3) 205–211.

World Health Organization (2007) *Global Age-friendly Cities: A guide* [online]. Available at: http://www.who.int/ageing/publications/Global_age_friendly_cities_Guide_English.pdf (accessed January 2015).

Chapter 10: The future for mental health services: some possibilities

By Simon Lawton-Smith

'No man is an island entire of itself; every man
is a piece of the continent, a part of the main.'

John Donne (1572–1631), Meditation XVII, *Devotions Upon Emergent Occasions*

John Donne's devotional words ring as true today as they did some 400 years ago, not least as a result of our greater understanding of the negative emotional impact on individuals of isolation from society, family and friends, and the dangers of loneliness to both physical and mental health. At the same time, our lives and our mental health are inextricably bound to others', and any one individual's difficulties impact on wider society.

If we change 'man' to 'mental health service', then we have the same truth: no mental health service is an island entire of itself; every mental health service is a piece of the continent, a part of the main. This needs to be acknowledged in all thinking about how mental health services should develop in the future, both in terms of policy and practice.

But what do we mean by 'mental health services'? In an NHS and UK context, the Mental Health Foundation has suggested the following definition:

'... services commissioned by NHS and local authority commissioners, provided by NHS, independent and voluntary sector services and local authority social services, in support of any person as a result of that person being assessed and diagnosed as having a mental disorder'. (2013a, p8)

While this omits privately commissioned and provided services, it does cover the bulk of service activity in the UK. Of course all four constituent countries of the UK have NHS and local authority provision of mental health support; however, given that health is a politically devolved issue, the detail of service structure, accountability, funding, commissioning, provision and law varies across them.

A mental health service may be many things – a consultation with a GP about feeling anxious or depressed; a course of psychotherapy; support provided in a person's own home by a community mental health team; inpatient care; psychiatric liaison services; mental health promotion activity, including, for example, gardening and sports projects; prison in-reach services; perinatal and child and adolescent mental health services. But it is important to recognise that much vital support for people with a mental illness comes through both physical healthcare services and non-health-related services such as welfare benefits and housing, with which mental health services need to work closely and collaboratively.

Looking to the past

The days of public mental health services effectively comprising isolated asylums set in the countryside and surrounded by high walls have long gone. The overriding trend of the past 50 years within UK mental health services, which continues to this day, has been deinstitutionalisation. A number of factors have played a role in this, not least the growing costs of asylums and inpatient care, the disclosure of scandals within their walls, the development of drugs that allow patients' worst symptoms to be controlled while they live in the community, and a growing social and ethical push towards treating people with a mental disorder as citizens with equal rights. Publicly funded psychiatric bed numbers across the UK have fallen from some 150,000 in the 1950s to fewer than 30,000 today.

Visions for the future

We are not short of ambitious visions for the future of mental health services in the UK. Indeed, there is a good deal of agreement about what mental health services should look like as we move through the 21st century. Amalgamated below are some of the main themes running through a number of published visions (Strong, 2000; Sainsbury Centre for Mental Health, 2006; Future Vision Coalition, 2009; Northern Ireland Executive, 2012; Welsh Government, 2012; Scottish Government, 2012; Mental Health Foundation, 2013a; 2013b; Department of Health, 2014; NHS Confederation, 2014; CentreForum, 2014).

- Mental and emotional well-being will be a concern of all governments and public services, and the mental health of the whole population will be protected and improved. Mental health promotion and education will flourish, in particular in schools (see Chapter 4) and the workplace (see Chapter 7), and societal inequalities, which play a major role in the development of mental illness, will be reduced.

- Mental health will be taken as seriously as physical health, with inequalities in service provision and access, funding, quality of care and outcome between the two removed (for more on parity of esteem, see Chapter 6). To tackle high levels of comorbidity, the physical health of people with mental health conditions will be a priority. Mental health care and physical health care will be better integrated at every level.

- Governments will lead efforts to combat prejudices about mental health and stamp out discrimination faced by people with mental health problems. There will be accurate and responsible reporting of mental health issues.

- A true partnership will be established between health and social care professionals and patients and their families, who will have a say in service design and provision. People with mental health problems will be able to exercise control over their own healthcare. A range of effective, evidence-based care and support services will be offered to them.

- Service provision will be integrated through partnerships between national and local government, the NHS, other public services, and the independent and voluntary sectors. Innovation will come from working together, with each sector adding its talents and resources to tackle shared problems.

- Mental health information and support will be more fully integrated into the community, and be widely available in, among other places, GP surgeries, schools, libraries and workplaces.

- Primary care, and in particular GPs, will grow more expert in identifying and treating mental health problems, and both generic and specialist mental health care will be available in primary care settings.

- Hospitals will offer 'asylum in the true sense of the word'. They will provide a calm, restorative environment with a range of therapeutic activities for patients. There will be more crisis provision in the community, as an alternative to hospital.

- Services will adopt the recovery model, where people experiencing mental health difficulties are supported to make their lives better on their own terms. Those seeking work are supported into appropriate employment or other meaningful occupations and, once there, are offered ongoing support for as long as needed. In the criminal justice system there will be increasing support for people with a mental illness, such as court diversion and prison in-reach schemes.

- There will be continued investment in all-age mental health services, adequate to meet demand, not least in addressing infant and childhood mental health issues (see Chapters 3 and 4) and the challenge of increasing numbers of older people living with dementia and poor mental health (see Chapter 9).

- A wider range of effective, evidence-based, treatments will be available for people. There will be continuing research into pharmacological, neurological, psychological and social responses to mental illness. Evidence-based psychological therapies will be available to all who might benefit, including children and older people.

- Developments in new technology will benefit all people with mental health problems, in terms of increased self-management and delivery of services. It will also lead to better information systems within mental health services, compatible with other public service information systems.

- The future mental health workforce will consistently exhibit the necessary values, attitudes, skills and collaborative practice for treating and supporting individuals of all ages with mental health problems. It will include more 'peer workers', with lived experience of mental health problems. There will be a better understanding of the challenges facing staff trying to provide an expert service in often very challenging and demanding circumstances, and increased support for staff themselves, with appropriate status, manageable caseloads and minimal bureaucracy.

The Mental Health Foundation summed up what people want current and future mental health services to look like:

'holistic / integrated and multidisciplinary / local / community-based / person-centred / easy to access / early to intervene / recovery-based / and co-produced with service users and carers.'
(Mental Health Foundation, 2013a, p13)

The Department of Health in England has indicated that in future 'everyone who needs mental health care should get the right support, at the right time' (Department of Health, 2014, p4). In Wales, the government has talked of the need to form 'a single, seamless, comprehensive system for addressing mental health needs across all ages' (Welsh Government, 2012, p1). The Scottish Government has particularly focused on the greater future involvement of people who use mental health services:

'We must take a step into the future and think beyond how services are currently structured and delivered ... Self-help, self-referral, self-directed, self-management and peer to peer are all concepts that will only grow in

importance and which demand a different mindset and approach to service design. The system of the future must develop to embrace and adopt these approaches alongside the more traditional approaches to service delivery, which will also continue to be necessary'. (Scottish Government, 2012, p1)

Future challenges

These are fine words and fine ambitions, but there are significant challenges, not least in the form of pressures on resources. At the time of writing, the UK economy is still coming out of a period of recession and pressures on public spending have been, and still are, prominent. In England, the Nuffield Trust has stated that:

'Cost pressures on the NHS are projected to grow at around four per cent a year up to 2021/22 … If NHS funding is held flat in real terms beyond this spending review period, the NHS in England could experience a funding gap worth between £44 and £54 billion in 2021/22, unless offsetting productivity gains can be delivered.' (Nuffield Trust, 2012, p2)

Clearly, NHS and local authority-funded mental health services are as much at risk due to cost constraints as any other public service, and similar cost pressures will apply across the UK for the foreseeable future.

Second, demand for mental health services continues to increase, along with the expectations of people who use mental health services and their carers. Over the past 20–30 years, the UK has experienced a persistently high recorded level of psychiatric morbidity. Data from the English Adult Psychiatric Morbidity Survey of 2007 (NHS Health & Social Care Information Centre, 2009) indicated that nearly one person in four (23%) in England had at least one psychiatric disorder and 7.2% had two or more disorders. In addition, the Royal College of Psychiatrists (2013) has identified that one in 10 children and young people has a diagnosable mental disorder. With an estimated eight million more adults in the UK by 2030, and one million more children, this suggests that in 15 years' time there will be some two million more adults and 100,000 more children with mental health problems in the UK than today.

Third, there appears to be an increasing level of (or at least a better recognition of) comorbidity and multiple morbidity involving people with both significant physical and mental health needs. These needs can be complex and interrelated, requiring new approaches to integrated care.

What needs to happen

Despite these and other challenges, there are reasons to be optimistic about the future of mental health services. The story of the past 50 years has generally been a positive one, and it is reasonable to assume that the next 50 years will see further improvements, not least through technological advances in care and treatment. However, this requires planned, concerted activity and effort from a wide range of stakeholders, all the way from national governments down to individual patients.

Below is just a brief summary of some of the key areas where work needs to be driven forward.

Public mental health

Given the expected increase in demand on mental health services simply through demographic changes, it will be essential to invest more in promoting public mental health. Indeed, a reduction in the number of people across the UK developing mental disorders is arguably the only way that mental health services will adequately cope with demand in 20 or 30 years' time. Many forms of prevention and early intervention show outstandingly good value for money, saving public expenditure as well as radically improving the quality of people's lives (Centre for Mental Health, 2011) (see Chapters 3, 4 and 12 for more information). Further research into what works is necessary, and the evidence needs to be widely understood both by the general public and all healthcare staff.

Resources

We can hope for improved efficiency within mental health services – providing more services for less money, at no cost to quality – but few believe that this alone will tackle tomorrow's demands. Will extra revenue come from higher levels of taxation and health spending? An expansion of charging for some NHS services, such as with prescription charges and dental fees? A limit on what can be provided through the NHS? A wider role for health insurance schemes?

The NHS Confederation has called for a public debate on where future investment in mental health services will come from (NHS Confederation, 2014). It is up to governments across the UK to initiate that debate.

As for what services people are able to access, whoever has the responsibility for commissioning across the different UK health systems will need an in-depth understanding of the challenges posed by poor mental health, both nationally and in local communities, and the evidence-base around the most effective interventions and treatments. This requires specialist mental health commissioning skills.

Research

We have thankfully come a long way from the world of straightjackets, cold baths and lobotomies. However, while there have been significant improvements in treatment through, primarily, newer and more effective medication and talking therapies, there is still an imbalance between the relatively low level of investment into researching new treatments and interventions, and the high health, social and economic burden of disease caused by mental illness. This imbalance must be rectified.

Recovery and personalisation

All mental health services, wherever provided, need to adopt the 'recovery model' of care, supporting people to build lives for themselves, rather than simply providing clinical treatment. They also need to practise a collaborative, personalised approach to patients/clients. Many do already, of course, and this is reflected in better outcomes and higher levels of patient satisfaction. These approaches and values need to be built into the core training of all health and social care staff, and their continuing professional development.

Self-management

Given current and future resource pressures on services, we would do well to increase patients' capacity to self-manage their conditions safely. The future should see people becoming increasingly responsible for their own care, where possible. This will involve educating patients in issues such as adherence to prescribed medication, managing a comorbid physical health problem, or improving diet and exercise regimes. There will be a significant role for new technology in this to allow patients quick access to information and advice. (For an example of self-management and peer support, see Chapter 12.)

Integrated care

There has long been an understanding of the benefits of integrating care across boundaries, for example between primary and secondary care, or between physical and mental healthcare. Research has identified a range of structural arrangements that can help to establish effective integrated care for people with mental health needs (Mental Health Foundation, 2013b). These include:

- information-sharing systems compatible within and across different organisations
- shared protocols and partnership agreements within and between organisations
- the ability to pool funds from different funding streams into a single integrated care budget
- the co-location of services, multidisciplinary teams and liaison services.

However, at the end of the day it is people and relationships rather than structural arrangements that ultimately make or break good integrated care. The future of effective integrated care therefore lies primarily in recruiting, training, maintaining and developing a workforce in both health and social care that is passionate and committed to the principles and practice of holistic care and partnership working.

Mental health in primary care

Remaining on the theme of integration, there is general agreement that mental health services should be fully integrated into primary care (World Health Organization, 2007). In the UK, many GPs have a good knowledge of mental health issues, but not all of them. Ninety per cent of people with mental health problems across the lifespan are managed in primary care, and the Royal College of General Practitioners has some strong messages about the need for GPs to address mental health among their patients (Royal College of General Practitioners, 2014). However, it is essential in the future to remove variations in the quality of care that people get at primary care level.

All the evidence suggests that early intervention, regardless of age or diagnosis, improves outcomes, and primary care is where most mental health problems are likely to be first identified. Yet most investment is in late intervention at very high cost. GPs of the future need to become leaders in mental health care. This does not mean they need to become mental health specialists, but they need to know as much about mental health as they do about physical health, to understand the way each impacts on the other, and the costs of comorbidity (King's Fund, 2012). At the same time, we should be looking for specialist mental health services to make themselves routinely available in primary care and community settings.

Hospital and crisis care

It is difficult, regrettably, to imagine a future without some form of inpatient care for people with severe mental illness when they are very unwell. Despite much excellent inpatient care today, criticism exists particularly around inpatient environments and regimes being untherapeutic, often with patients having very little to occupy themselves, a situation exacerbated by high occupancy levels and pressures on staff time. It has been proved possible to develop inpatient services that are recovery-focused and stimulating (Star Wards, 2014; Royal College of Psychiatrists, 2014), but it will require continuous effort and commitment to carry this forward into the future.

Of course we should be looking to offer people in crisis alternatives to a hospital admission where possible. There are some good examples of such services in the UK, but they are patchy and under pressure from both demand and financial constraints. Helpfully, the recent Mental Health Crisis Care concordat in England (Department of Health & Home Office, 2014) talks both about preventing crises, and managing them when they happen. However, a concordat is only a piece of paper – if future mental health services are to meet people's needs in a crisis, then all the signatories to the concordat, and in particular commissioners of the relevant services, need to know what good practice is, and discuss with patients and their carers how it can be implemented more widely.

Workforce

None of the above, of course, is possible without 'bold leadership' (NHS Confederation, 2014) and the right staff. The mental health workforce of the future needs a balance of specialist and generalist staff with clearly defined skills and roles that is able and willing to work collaboratively in support of individual patients. It will be important not to water down the specialist skills that at times mentally ill people both need and want, but there will very likely be an increasing role for primary care staff, peer support workers and 'navigators' who can help people find their way through the complex healthcare and social support systems they rely on.

Alongside a specialist workforce, though, we also need to see increased knowledge and understanding of mental health issues among all health and social care staff, and particularly GPs. The indivisibility of physical and mental health should be a core element of all health and social care basic training, along with an expansion of cross-boundary inter-professional training and education. We must also make sure that staff are allowed to do the job they are trained for. This means according them the status and rewards appropriate to their work, providing opportunities to learn and develop new skills, providing adequate supervision and resources, and offering them an attractive career path.

Conclusion

Mental illness has, it seems, always been part of the human condition, though viewed differently across time and cultures. In 1887, the first Annual Report of the

After-care Association for Poor and Friendless Female Convalescents on Leaving Asylums for the Insane (today's mental health charity Together), noted that:

'the work undertaken by the society can never be expected to become very popular in the strict sense of the word, but there is scarcely no work more needed and the Association is the only one that offers help for those people recovering from perhaps the worst of ailments. The sad trial of insanity.'

(Strong, 2000, p11)

Despite many advances in care and treatment, we are frustratingly distant from eradicating this 'sad trial of insanity' from our lives. We are, however, considerably more enlightened about treatment and prevention of a range of mental disorders today than we were 50, 20 or even 10 years ago. With advances in research and technology that at present we can only dream of, we can expect to become even more enlightened as the 21st century progresses.

However, this will not happen by itself. Politicians, commissioners of services and mental health and wider healthcare professions need to be relentless in driving improvement to services. It goes without saying that, whatever efficiencies may be achieved, there must be an investment of resources across the UK that is appropriate to the burden of mental illness. Alongside this, policy and practice must be underpinned by a focus on prevention, early intervention, personalisation, self-management, recovery, collaboration and partnership. Only then will mental health services become truly 'fit for the future'.

References

Centre for Mental Health (2011) *Mental Health Promotion and Mental Illness Prevention: The economic case* [online]. London: Centre for Mental Health. Available at: http://www.centreformentalhealth.org.uk/publications/mental_health_promotion_economic_case.aspx?ID=630 (accessed December 2014).

CentreForum (2014) *The Pursuit of Happiness: A new ambition for our mental health* [online]. London: CentreForum. Available at: http://www.centreforum.org/assets/pubs/the-pursuit-of-happiness.pdf (accessed December 2014).

Department of Health (2014) *Closing the Gap: Priorities for essential change in mental health [online]*. London: Department of Health. Available at: https://www.gov.uk/government/publications/mental-health-priorities-for-change (accessed December 2014).

Department of Health & Home Office (2014) *Mental Health Crisis Care Concordat: Improving outcomes for people experiencing mental health crisis* [online]. London: HM Government. Available at: https://www.gov.uk/government/uploads/system/uploads/attachment_data/file/281242/36353_Mental_Health_Crisis_accessible.pdf (accessed December 2014).

Future Vision Coalition (2009) *A Future Vision for Mental Health* [online]. London: NHS Confederation. Available at: http://www.nhsconfed.org/Publications/reports/Pages/A-future-vision-for-mental-health.aspx (Accessed December 2014).

King's Fund (2012) *Long Term Conditions and Mental Health: The cost of co-morbidities* [online]. London: King's Fund. Available at: http://www.kingsfund.org.uk/sites/files/kf/field/field_publication_ file/long-term-conditions-mental-health-cost-comorbidities-naylor-feb12.pdf (accessed December 2014).

Mental Health Foundation (2013a) *Starting Today: The future of mental health services* [online]. London: Mental Health Foundation. Available at: http://www.mentalhealth.org.uk/publications/ starting-today-future-of-mental-health-services/ (accessed December 2014).

Mental Health Foundation (2013b) *Crossing Boundaries: Improving integrated care for people with mental health problems* [online]. London: Mental Health Foundation. Available at: http://www. mentalhealth.org.uk/publications/crossing-boundaries/ (accessed December 2014).

NHS Confederation (2014) *The Future of Mental Health. Discussion paper, March 2014, Issue 16.* London: NHS Confederation. Available at: http://www.nhsconfed.org/Publications/discussion-paper/ Pages/mhn-2014-future-of-mental-health.aspx (accessed December 2014).

NHS Health & Social Care Information Centre (2009) *Adult Psychiatric Morbidity Survey 2007* [online]. Leeds: NHS Health and Social Care Information Centre. Available at: http://www.hscic.gov.uk/ pubs/psychiatricmorbidity07 (accessed December 2014).

Northern Ireland Executive (2012) *Delivering the Bamford Vision: The response of the Northern Ireland Executive to the Bamford Review of Mental Health and Learning Disability. Action Plan 2012–15* [online]. Belfast: Northern Ireland Executive. Available at: http://www.dhsspsni.gov.uk/2012- 2015-bamford-action-plan.pdf (accessed December 2014).

Nuffield Trust (2012) *A Decade of Austerity* [online]. London: Nuffield Trust. Available at: http://www. nuffieldtrust.org.uk/publications/decade-austerity-funding-pressures-facing-nhs (accessed December 2014).

Royal College of General Practitioners (2014) *RCGP Curriculum*. London: Royal College of General Practitioners. Available at: http://www.rcgp.org.uk/gp-training-and-exams/~/media/Files/GP-training- and-exams/Curriculum-2012/RCGP-Curriculum-3-10-Mental-Health-Problems.ashx (accessed December 2014).

Royal College of Psychiatrists (2013) *Briefing on Child and Adolescent In-patient Mental Health Services Commons Adjournment Debate – 23 October 2013* [online]. London: Royal College of Psychiatrists. Available at: http://www.rcpsych.ac.uk/pdf/CAMHS%20debate%20briefing%20-%20 Oct%202013.pdf (accessed December 2014).

Royal College of Psychiatrists (2014) *Accreditation for Inpatient Mental Health Services (AIMS)* [online]. London: Royal College of Psychiatrists. Available at: http://www.rcpsych.ac.uk/ workinpsychiatry/qualityimprovement/qualityandaccreditation/psychiatricwards/aims.aspx (accessed December 2014).

Sainsbury Centre for Mental Health (2006) *The Future of Mental Health: A vision for 2015* [online]. London: Centre for Mental Health. Available at: http://www.centreformentalhealth.org.uk/pdfs/mental_ health_futures_policy_paper.pdf (accessed December 2014).

Scottish Government (2012) *Mental Health Strategy for Scotland: 2012–2015* [online]. Edinburgh: Scottish Government. Available at: http://www.scotland.gov.uk/Publications/2012/08/9714/0 (accessed December 2014).

Star Wards (2014) *Star Wards: Inspiring mental health inpatient care* [online]. Available at: http:// starwards.org.uk/ (accessed December 2014).

Strong (2000) *Community Care in the Making: A history of MACA 1879–2000*. London: Together.

Welsh Government (2012) *Together for Mental Health: A cross-government strategy for mental health and wellbeing in Wales* [online]. Cardiff: Welsh Government. Available at: http://wales.gov.uk/ consultations/healthsocialcare/mhealth/?lang=en (accessed December 2014).

World Health Organization (2007) *Integrating Mental Health Services Into Primary Health Care* [online]. Geneva: World Health Organization. Available at: http://www.who.int/mental_health/policy/ services/3_MHintoPHC_Infosheet.pdf (accessed December 2014).

Chapter 11:
Digital: reality

By Chris O'Sullivan and Mark Brown

There are few, if any, areas of human endeavour in the Western world that have not been affected by the growth of digital technologies. From visiting a cash machine to sending an email, they have changed the way in which industries function and the ways in which we make use of them. Digital technologies have been changing our lives for over 60 years. For many of us the arrival of widespread internet access, the growth of mobile devices such as smartphones and tablets, and ever-increasing computing power at lower prices has changed more elements of our work, home and social lives than some of us would care to admit.

Even mental health is not exempt from the process described by Andrew McAfee (2014), co-author of *The Second Machine Age*, as 'digital encroachment' – the replacement of human labour with digital or machine labour. Though there are indisputable challenges with equality of access and skills to use technology, the risks and opportunities of the digital world are part of life for many people who experience mental health difficulties.

The 'industry' of supporting people with mental health difficulties, dealing as it does with human interactions, is unlikely to be replaced by solely digital services. The question is: how can we best harness the possibilities of digital technologies to make the care, support and enablement of people who are experiencing mental health problems the most effective it can be?

Understanding and meeting the needs of digital natives

Many people assume that the archetypal user of the internet is a young person with a laptop. Much has been made of the needs of 'digital natives' (Prensky, 2001) – those born after 1987 for whom digital has been a reality throughout their lives. These days the role of personal devices like smartphones and tablets is key for young people, but static devices like games consoles and laptops are also a big part of young people's digital lives.

In many respects, this generation will be at the vanguard of demanding technology-based solutions as their need for public service involvement collides with their unwillingness to accept services that don't recognise that they lead lives where online and offline activity interweave seamlessly. Some of the most established UK examples of innovation in digital mental health have been developed for or with young people, but it's worth remembering that the archetypal 'young people with laptops' are now, in the second decade of the 21st century, in their early to mid-thirties. Much of the evidence base regarding young people's current use of digital technology has been developed in Australia by the Young and Well Cooperative Research Centre[7], with publications of global interest on topics such as risk, gaming and mental health, co-production, and on the mental health improvement aspects of social media. Collin *et al* (2011) conducted a literature review into the positive aspects of online social networking for young people. They suggested that the collaborative, creative and social capital aspects of digital technology can be important in young people's mental well-being, and that those most at risk and who are most likely to be excluded can have the most to gain. Equally, they proposed a broader approach to managing risk through digital citizenship work to ensure respect and awareness of risks.

Innovation Labs and Project 99 are examples of initiatives in this field.

Project 99

NHS Greater Glasgow and Clyde is Scotland's largest health board. Working with community planning partners, it has a Strategic Framework for Child and Youth Mental Health Improvement which recognises the role of digital technology as a communication medium and a setting for a range of actions in young people's lives.

In 2013 the health board commissioned a consortium bringing together national youth information charity Young Scot with the Mental Health Foundation and service design agency Snook, to work with board staff, young people and a multi-agency steering group to explore ways in which the board could engage with young people on digital mental health. The project, named Project 99 by young people, used co-design approaches to develop basic prototypes of digital tools to address challenges young people raised.

In the scoping phase, a rapid review of literature was accompanied by a map of current digital tools for young people's mental health. Sixty active and developing

---

7   For more information, see www.youngandwellcrc.org.au

digital mental health assets were described using a mapping framework that oriented them both by audience of young people (using a whole population approach) and by the type of asset/activity offered. This included assets from across the UK and beyond, and was a snapshot in time in mid-2013. Three principal 'activity types' were proposed:

- Technology for information: where young people seek information about mental health and distress using the internet or digital technology.

- Technology for service delivery: where young people access e-health services (services delivered using digital methods), or use technology to engage with or prepare for engagement with services.

- Technology for social connection, identity and self-realisation: where young people use technology to curate their experience, offer and receive peer support, explore their identities, collaborate and share content.

Work directly with young people yielded rich insights for in-depth case studies of how local young people led their digital lives. Equally, when supported to engage in design workshops, young people proposed solutions to challenges that were in equal part imaginative and pragmatic. They gave a range of design insights, including suggesting that digital tools should use humour where appropriate, and should be 'beautiful' enough to encourage users to take responsibility for the spaces and take pride in their engagement.

The co-design groups were clear that a digital 'springboard' that would allow a range of existing resources to be highlighted within a health board 'approved' site would allow resources to be accessed easily, and could improve perceptions of validity in key groups such as health and education staff. Young people also highlighted the need to support friends in distress. From this, Support Squared was proposed, a graphic digital product to facilitate support for friends dealing with peer distress. All of the ideas and insights developed by Project 99 are free for others to build upon and use, based on a Creative Commons license.

The development groundwork laid down by Project 99 is being taken forward through the award of a grant under the EU 7th Research Framework Project CHEST[8], which exists to fund digital innovation to address social challenges. Through this funding, several of the prototype ideas co-designed with young people will be developed into viable products for scaling in the board area.

For more information, see the Project 99 full report at: www.wegot99.com

---

8   For more information, see www.chest-project.eu

Innovation Labs

Innovation Labs was a project initially conceived in 2011 by the board of a national young people's mental health and well-being project, Right Here – a five-year joint action learning project between the Paul Hamlyn Foundation and the Mental Health Foundation. Right Here supported four partnerships across England and Northern Ireland to enable young people to engage directly in the development of mental health services and activities to promote their mental health. The focus of Right Here was on the 16–25 age group.

The Innovation Labs were structured as a three-stage process, and the idea was to come up with a number of digital projects to support young people's mental health and well-being. At each stage there was a mixture of young people (with and without experience of mental health difficulty), youth work professionals, mental health professionals and people who work in tech industries.

Critical to the development of the Innovation Lab's programme was the involvement of a range of mental health organisations, digital specialists and three of the UK's leading funders in the shape of Comic Relief, Nominet Trust and the Paul Hamlyn Foundation.

The initial model was the 'hack day', or 'hackathon'. Hackathons rose to prominence in the early to mid-2000s among US software development companies and involved bringing together software designers, graphic designers, interface designers and others to quickly develop new pieces of software. The idea is to get people together to come up with a finished piece of software at the end of the day (or days).

After an initial event with young people, mental health professionals and youth work professionals to explore the opportunities and challenges of such an intense method of engagement, it was decided that a modified hackathon format for young people with experience of mental health difficulty would be a viable proposition.

Right Here invited applications to deliver two 'Innovation Labs': the first to develop a broad range of ideas and the second to hone those ideas into briefs that could then be developed as actual young people's digital projects[9]. A difficulty with consultation events in general, but technology-based events in particular, is that often people either do not have enough awareness of existing technology and existing projects and so suggest ideas that are already in existence, or they turn up with very fixed ideas for projects based on things that they have already seen or experienced. Both of these mean that the process can misidentify actual problems that could successfully be solved using technological means.

---

9   For more information, see www.innovationlabs.org.uk

The first Innovation Lab developed a range of ideas or problems. These were examined and voted upon and a second Lab was held to further focus people on certain selected ideas or areas. During the second Lab, ideas were worked up to the point where they had a defined user in mind, establishing what need the tool would meet and a notion of the mechanism by which the tool might function. These ideas were then pitched by young people to a panel of decision makers.

The funders (Comic Relief, Paul Hamlyn Foundation and Nominet Trust) commissioned full technical specifications for eight projects, and a project board, which consisted of funders, Right Here partners and young people, selected the successful consortia and managed the grant programme. Six projects were funded to launch in a process managed by Comic Relief. Innovation Labs also funded ongoing support for learning and development from the process, resulting in 70 blog posts on the Lab's website, a popular newsletter and the publication of an ebook (Boardwell & Roberson, 2014). A process evaluation of the Labs was undertaken (Boon, 2013) and a wider impact evaluation of the apps and tools is currently being undertaken.

All of the projects commissioned launched a 'minimum viable product' by July 2014. The tools launched addressed a range of problems, spanning all domains of life from specific challenges in accessing services and self-management, to skills such as relationships and employment. The solutions that were developed included websites and mobile apps in iOS and Android formats.

The six Innovation Labs projects were:

- **Doc Ready:** a website that helps young people feel more confident and get better results when they see their GP about a mental health issue. Available at www.docready.org

- **HeadMeds:** a website that provides accessible, straight-talking information on young people's mental health medication. Available at www.headmeds.org.uk

- **InHand:** a digital friend that provides young people with tools, advice and activities when their mental health is at risk. Available at www.inhand.org.uk

- **Well Informed:** a place for the children and young people's workforce to go to get instant, accurate support on youth mental health. Available at www.wellinformed.org.uk

- **Moodbug:** a tool for people to share how they feel with their close friends and let them know when they're thinking about them. Available at www.moodbug.me

- **Madly in Love:** a relationship and mental health advice site for young people and their partners. Available at www.madlyinlove.org.uk

- **Find Get Give:** enables young people to find mental health support in their area and give feedback on it. Available at www.findgetgive.com

Doc Ready exemplifies the Lab's approach of developing tools that meet the needs expressed by young people. Young people in the Lab's process identified GP consultations around mental health as difficult experiences where they felt that they weren't being understood. Doc Ready is a simple web-based app that uses prompts to help young people to create a checklist of things that they want to talk to their GP about in relation to their mental health.

The app generates the checklist of experiences and feelings which can be reordered and added to, and which can be printed, emailed or saved as a pdf file. The user can then take this list to their consultation. The app does not store any data and works from any internet browser as young people indicated they did not want their data to be stored and did not want to download an app that might be seen by others.

The initial ideas generated looked at modifying the behaviour of GPs. The development process of Doc Ready pivoted this, knowing it would be difficult to influence GPs to adopt such a tool, to become an application that would remove some of the challenges young people faced in these difficult initial consultations.

The app itself can easily be embedded in any third-party website, giving organisations that work with young people a way to help and support them to access their GP.

Ensuring the inclusion of 'digital immigrants' and 'digital refugees'

There is a growing population of people who experience mental distress or mental health problems who use online communication as the primary method of discussing and seeking solutions to this distress. Prensky (2001) describes a population of 'digital immigrants' – people born before the digital natives but who have taken to using technology. Where decision makers and mental health professionals use their awareness of technology as a potential force for good in mental health, digital champions can emerge and model innovation and adoption of technology in a range of settings.

Project Ginsberg and mHealth Habitat (pp123–124) look to the wider population. People already use digital technologies to self-manage and self-define in online campaigning activities that carry into life. Further work to develop and widen uptake of such activities has potential both for reducing the pressure on primary care services and increasing the reach of social movements to address stigma.

Increasingly, we are also seeing the emergence of populations of 'digital refugees' – people with shared experiences forming digital communities of interest that provide more accessible routes to peer support and building social capital than face-to-face interaction. This population is especially critical of existing services seeking to colonise online community spaces as the internet is, for them, a safe space for which they don't have an offline analogue.

mHealthHabitat Leeds

Victoria Betton is the founder and leader of mHealthHabitat[10], 'a programme funded within the NHS which aspires to create a habitat in Leeds where mHealth [digital health] can flourish'.

She says of the current situation within the NHS regarding digital solutions:

'We are finding that there are plenty of mental health professionals who understand the potential to innovate and they are keen for digital to play a part in enabling people to take control of their mental health and well-being. However, they are not sure where to start and the barriers of information technology and information governance seem like hurdles which are just too big to overcome. They tell us that having a team who are within the NHS family but with connections with the external developer and designer community is invaluable.'

(Betton & Tomlinson, 2013)

Betton recognises that while the imperative to explore digital products is strong, at present the NHS does not always have the understanding, contacts or thinking to develop digital products or services well. mHealthHabitat helps people who need to access services, and clinicians, to explore what problems they face and to assess whether digital can be part of the solution. They provide a space in which people, with the help of individuals with digital skills and expertise, can find solutions and overcome barriers such as policies, procedures, information technology, information governance and funding. Key to the approach is bringing together different communities, including designers and developers with health staff and people with lived experience and professionals. These connections enable a wide range of partnerships, business cases and grant applications to be developed, and for learning to be shared.

---

10 For more information, see www.mhealthhabitat.co.uk

mHealthHabitat reflects a growing understanding that digital solutions in health are less about off-the-shelf procurement or commissioning and more about a complex interplay between a user's wishes, needs and preferences, and the knowledge and expertise to develop solutions that meet organisational aims. This process requires a way of working that feels new or unusual to people already working in and around mental health but which can make it easier to execute ideas such as co-production and the efficient direction of resources to meet users' needs.

Project Ginsberg

In its *Mental Health Strategy for Scotland 2012–2015*, the Scottish Government included among its commitments:

> '*Commitment 6: During the period of the Mental Health Strategy we will develop a Scotland-wide approach to improving mental health through new technology in collaboration with NHS 24.*'

(Scottish Government, 2012)

As part of this undertaking the Scottish Government began work with NHS 24 and New Media Scotland to explore the development of a new digital platform to enable people who use digital technology in relation to their health to better self-manage distress, in whatever form. Project Ginsberg[11] was formed using an agile development approach (Beck *et al*, 2001) to create a 'tech start-up' business model within the framework of government and the NHS. The project aims to create a platform to enable users to gather insights about themselves by answering three key questions about their well-being daily, and relating this to data gathered on nutrition, exercise, sleep, alcohol use, social media use and logged events.

A public beta of the first phase was launched in October 2014, with new features being added regularly following user feedback and 'development sprints'.

Critically, Ginsberg is intended to enable users to aggregate data about themselves confidentially and act upon the insights the relationships between the data provide. The platform creates connections, and does not intervene or direct. In time, new apps and resources will increase the detail and choice of information that can be integrated and received by the user.

The project is creating an entirely new type of digital tool in mental health at exactly the moment when personal health tracking and self-management is growing. This type of emergent approach, creating a novel and uniquely digital

---

11 For more information, see https://www.ginsberg.io

resource for a population that knows and uses digital freely is likely to be of great interest in coming years.

Digital innovation in public and third sectors

At the time of writing, the impact of digital technology on mental health has been more potential than actual. In her annual report, Chief Medical Officer for England Sally Davies stresses the potential for digital technologies to change mental health:

> *'Technology offers the potential to transform mental healthcare delivery through widening access to information and services, offering adherence support and real-time symptom monitoring that allows earlier and more timely interventions and new treatments such as non-invasive neuromodulation for depression and psychosis. Advances in sensor technology, on-line psychological therapy and remote video consultation, mobile apps and gaming represent real opportunities to engage and empower patients with mental health problems.'*

(Davies, 2014)

The challenge we face in mental health is to move beyond the idea that digital projects are mainly websites – digital vehicles for conveying information – and move to viewing them as closer to digital tools or services that help people do things they want or need to do. If we work within mental health then our specialism is mental health, not the engineering of digital tools.

Too often mental health services have tried to commission the final form of a tool to solve a problem without first commissioning the process to discover what the correct solution to that problem is. This 'app blindness' often means that digital solutions are commissioned without understanding the needs and wishes of those who will use them or the problems they seek to address.

The objective for digital projects in mental health must be to create tools, services, apps or devices that meet a defined objective, function in a way that fits the needs, wishes and preferences of those that are intended to use them, and which do no harm regarding resources available for their development, deployment and continued maintenance and upkeep. In UK mental health the sector has traditionally worked on the basis of commissioning services on behalf of patients or service users. This has led to situations where the decisions by commissioners are made upon an assessment of need derived from many competing demands:

organisational, financial, strategic, clinical, political. In this mix of competing stakeholder interests it can be easy to lose sight of the fact that apps and digital tools are things that people use to make something happen. 'App blindness' can occur when pressure to have or develop an app without adequate understanding of the audience, problem or technical requirement results in the development of a tool which isn't used, doesn't add social value, and is not financially viable or sustainable (Nominet Trust, 2014). A screwdriver with a grip that doesn't feel right in your hand is a screwdriver you leave in the drawer. As with physical tools, so with digital ones.

Making a successful digital tool therefore requires thinking about users, their needs and their preferences, as well as thinking about the requirements of stakeholders. A failure to recognise these varying needs risks the development of a 'reverse inequality' where a reticence to act due to concerns about access for some leads to the exclusion of others. Digital isn't the answer for everyone, and indeed assuming people have digital access can damage digital adoption. But for some it is the first port of call, and for many it is at least part of the picture.

Equally, in taking a whole-population approach to prevention, we need to recognise not only that there is a role for technology at the sharp end of care and treatment, but also that the cultural, political and leisure opportunities afforded by the internet have the potential to support and develop individual and community well-being across the life course.

To date it has been uncomfortable for some to discuss the possibilities of using digital technologies to create better outcomes for people with mental health difficulties. The reasons for this have differed from organisation to organisation and area to area. For some it is a reflection of fears that mental health services will have their 'human face' eroded, for others it is the legacy of poor-quality implementation of information technology (IT) tools in clinical settings, while others may question the wisdom of spending limited funds on technological white elephants over 'tried and tested' methods or practices.

In mental health we have often been found wanting in our overall ability to provide services that actually fit the ways that people live their lives. In the development of digital tools this is the kiss of death. The reality, however, is that digital isn't going away. It is a mistake to assume that technology solutions are a panacea that can replace high-quality face-to-face interaction. But equally an unwillingness to explore digital opportunities and manage the barriers that inhibit digital innovation risks the creation of a new type of inequality where some people's digital lives are ignored or their primary communication method is not recognised.

Further reading

Brown M (2011) *On Spending a Saturday Innovating* [online]. Available at: http://www.oneinfourmag.org/index.php/on-spending-a-saturday-innovating/ (accessed April 2015).

Brown M (2012) *#Mindtech: Observations from a rooftop* [online]. Available at: http://www.oneinfourmag.org/index.php/mindtech-observations-from-a-rooftop/ (accessed April 2015).

Brown M (2013) *Blog Posts on Developing Doc Ready* [online]. Available at: http://www.innovationlabs.org.uk/author/markoneinfour/ (accessed April 2015).

Brown M (2014) *On Mental Health and Digital: Avoiding all or nothing, not knowing what to back and 'bigness'* [online]. Available at: http://thenewmentalhealth.org/?p=72 (accessed April 2015).

Brown M (2014) *The NHS Versus the Ghost of Failed IT Past* [online]. Available at: http://thenewmentalhealth.org/?p=100 (accessed April 2015).

Campbell AJ & Robards F (2013) *Using Technologies Safely and Effectively to Promote Young People's Wellbeing: A better practice guide for services* [online]. Abbotsford, Australia: NSW Centre for the Advancement of Adolescent Health. Westmead and the Young and Well CRC. Available at: http://reports.youngandwellcrc.org.au/a-better-practice-guide-for-services/ (accessed April 2015).

Hagen P, Collin P, Metcalf A, Nicholas M, Rahilly K & Swainston N (2012) *Participatory Design of Evidence-based Online Youth Mental Health Promotion, Prevention, Early Intervention and Treatment.* Melbourne, Australia: Young and Well Cooperative Research Centre.

Innovations Labs (2013) *Labs Innovation Process Evaluation 2010-12: What we learnt* (blog post) [online]. Available at: http://www.innovationlabs.org.uk/2013/07/24/innovation-process-learning/ (accessed April 2015).

Johnson D, Jones C, Scholes L & Carras M (2013) *Videogames and Wellbeing.* Melbourne: Young and Well Cooperative Research Centre.

NHS Greater Glasgow and Clyde (2013) *Project 99 Full Report* [online]. Available at: http://www.wegot99.com (accessed April 2015).

References

Beck *et al* (2001) *Manifesto for Agile Software Development.* Agile Alliance.

Betton V & Tomlinson V (2013) *Social Media in Mental Health Practice: Online network tools for recovery and living well* [online]. Leeds: Leeds and York Partnership NHS Foundation Trust. Available at: http://www.leedsandyorkpft.nhs.uk/professionals/digitalhealthinnovation (accessed February 2015).

Boardwell J & Roberson J (2014) *Learning From the Labs: How to fund and deliver social tech for charities and social enterprises.* EBook available to download free at http://www.innovationlabs.org.uk/2014/11/06/how-to-fund-and-deliver-social-tech/ (accessed February 2015).

Brynjolfson E & McAfee (2014) *The Second Machine Age.* New York: WW Norton.

Boon V (2013) Innovation Labs Process Evaluation: Dec 2010 – Feb 2012. London: Innovation Labs.

Collin P, Rahilly K, Richardson I & Third A (2011) *The Benefits of Social Networking Services: A literature review* [online]. Melbourne: Young and Well CRC. Available at: http://www.yawcrc.org.au/knowledge-hub/publications (accessed February 2015).

Davies SC (2014) *Annual Report of the Chief Medical Officer 2013, Public Mental Health Priorities: Investing in the evidence* [online]. London: Department of Health. Available at: https://www.gov.uk/government/publications/chief-medical-officer-cmo-annual-report-public-mental-health (accessed February 2015).

Nominet Trust (2014) *The Triple Helix Model for Social Innovation* [online]. Available at: http://www.nominettrust.org.uk/knowledge-centre/blogs/triple-helix-social-tech-innovation (accessed February 2015).

Prensky M (2001) Digital natives, digital immigrants. *On the Horizon* **9** (5) 1–6.

Scottish Government (2012) *Mental Health Strategy for Scotland 2012-2015* [online]. Edinburgh: Scottish Government. Available at: http://www.scotland.gov.uk/Publications/2012/08/9714 (accessed February 2015).

Chapter 12: Self-management and peer support: what makes it different, what makes it work

By David Crepaz-Keay

Illustrations by Jolie Goodman

Introduction

The Mental Health Foundation has developed, delivered and evaluated a self-management and peer support intervention for people who have used secondary mental health services. The development and delivery of this intervention have been described in detail elsewhere (Crepaz-Keay & Cyhlarova, 2012) and recent research has shown a significant positive impact on well-being and healthy behaviour (Cyhlarova *et al*, 2015) as well as a promising cost benefit analysis (Lemmi *et al*, 2015). The intervention has also recently won a Good Practice Award from Public Health Wales. Subsequent variations have been developed for people from black and minority ethnic (BME) communities, women, single parents and prisoners.

This chapter sets out in words and pictures some of our findings with a particular emphasis on the elements that make our approach to self-management different and effective.

The underlying values and principles

People have control

There are a variety of approaches to self-management, but what they all have in common is a desire to shift the locus of control from professionals or clinicians to the individuals themselves. Our approach to self-management is firmly based on the principle that people should be in as much control of their lives as possible.

This should be consistent with contemporary practice in mental health services, but control often remains in professional hands for people using secondary mental health services.

Life orientated, not condition orientated

An underlying principle of our approach is to focus on people's lives and minimise the negative impact that the condition, diagnosis or treatment has on individuals' lives.

Some self-management has a strong focus on managing a particular condition or illness, which will often involve ensuring people have a good understanding of the condition, its causes, symptoms and treatments, so that people can concentrate on reducing the risk of the most negative effects and responding quickly to difficulties where professional help is needed. This can be very effective for certain conditions, but we have found that where people do not accept or agree with a diagnosis and/or do not have effective treatments, a focus on a condition can be unhelpful.

People do not need to accept or believe the diagnosis they are given, they just need to want to minimise the impact that the perceived condition has on their life. Some people consider self-management to be complementary to existing services and others see it as an alternative; we do not subscribe exclusively to either view.

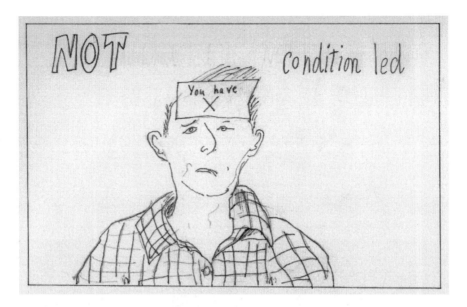

Asset/strength based

It follows from the first two principles that we believe that people have a lot to contribute to managing their mental (ill) health. The third key principle of our approach to self-management is that people have experience that can be turned into expertise, that people can acquire the skills to help themselves and each other.

People work together

The mental health services we grew up with were institutional in approach, even after the institutions closed, and people who used services for long periods became dependent. Many of the services that followed responded to this by encouraging people not to rely on support from others. People were treated as individuals and a significant goal became moving from dependence to independence. Many forms of self-management have the individual and their condition as the primary focus, and this is where our approach started. As the courses developed, it became clear that one of the primary benefits was the support people gave each other. This shifted our emphasis from self-management as an individual activity to self-management and peer support as a group activity. The objective changed from independence to interdependence – the idea that people are part of a community and that relationships between people are a key component of anyone's existence.

Every facilitator is a former participant

Some self-management interventions are clinician-led, some are expert patient-led, and while both approaches have potential, we settled on the latter, ensuring that all of our facilitators have been prior course participants. This helps to ensure continual development of the materials, gives the facilitators a strong sense of ownership and participants find it very encouraging that the people facilitating have shared the experience. We offer people support in the facilitation roles, such as project managers of self-management courses, who also have lived experience, debriefing facilitators after training and peer group sessions.

The key components

Self-help and self-management interventions have been used for many years, particularly in long-term physical health conditions. During this time, a wide variety of approaches has been described as self-management or self-help. Our version has three key ingredients: goal setting, problem solving and peer support.

Goal setting

Keeping a focus on what people can do, rather than what they can't, goal setting is the most important part of our approach. Goals can be modest or ambitious, or short, medium or long term, but they must be people's own goals, not set for them by others. More ambitious goals are broken down into smaller steps. Goals are recorded and shared, and monitoring progress towards goals is a very important part of the process.

Problem solving

Although just the process of articulating goals significantly increases our chances of achieving them, there can be many obstacles which prevent this. Some may be mental health related, some may be about discrimination and others could be unrelated to either. Overcoming the challenges through constructive problem solving is the next step in self-management.

Peer support

The problem solving isn't done in isolation – collective problem solving is the final part of our intervention. Our self-management training is delivered to a peer group of approximately 12 people, who work together through the training and ongoing support. There is a good chance that some of the problems will be known to other members of the group and some solution may already have been found. People also work together to solve some of the practical problems encountered, many of which are easier to solve as a team.

Some of the goals

With nearly 1,000 people taking part in our training the range of goals has been broad, but a number keep recurring:

- getting qualifications, volunteering or getting a job

- giving up smoking, losing weight or exercising more

- travelling, flying, learning to drive.

None of these goals are mental (ill) health-specific (though people have set mental health, condition-specific or treatment-orientated goals), and this reflects the focus on people's lives rather than their illness or diagnosis.

What people like

In addition to the measurable improvements in well-being and healthy behaviour outlined above, people have reported a number of other benefits of our work beyond achieving their own goals. We

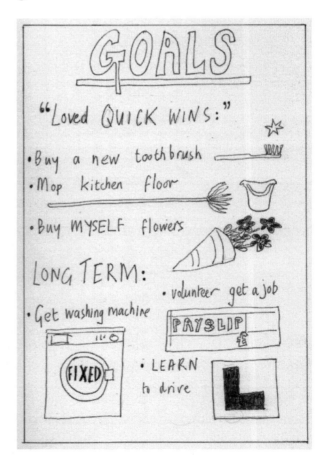

have highlighted two examples below because they seem to be less common in most approaches to mental ill-health.

A sense of achievement, learning from mistakes

Many people on our courses said that the professionals they had previously worked with (and sometimes their carers) were too protective. People can often learn from their mistakes and trying and failing is part of that learning. When this is done in a supportive environment it can be a very productive and rewarding process. People liked being stretched and pushed by their peers and said that they achieved more as a result.

Helping others

People with a psychiatric diagnosis usually find themselves cast in the role of help seekers in need of support. One of the most frequently reported benefits of our work is that of giving people the opportunity to help others. This, more than any other aspect, seems to underpin so many of the principles and values we are trying to achieve: focusing on strengths, working together, having something to offer, being neither dependent nor independent, but a valued member of the community.

How we have changed things

Our approach has developed over a few years now and we have learned much from our practice, participants and trainers. The original idea was to develop a 'schizophrenia equivalent' of the well-regarded self-management work developed by Bipolar UK (formerly the Manic Depression Fellowship). It soon became clear that people with a diagnosis of schizophrenia have a different relationship with their diagnosis and the focus changed to that described above. We originally planned to have a small number of expert trainers, but we discovered from participant feedback that the most effective trainers were those who they could identify with and felt they could emulate. Our ideal trainer seemed to be someone in a position that the participants thought they could achieve in six months.

What we plan next

We are currently working with a range of groups who we think can benefit from self-management and peer support including single parents, prisoners and people with a psychiatric diagnosis and physical health difficulties.

Acknowledgements

The development, delivery and evaluation of the self-management project was funded by the Big Lottery Fund. The courses and evaluation in South East London were funded by the Maudsley Charity. The authors would like to thank Kym Winstanley for the 'moving the goal posts' metaphor for self-management.

References

Crepaz-Keay D & Cyhlarova E (2012) A new self-management intervention for people with severe psychiatric diagnoses. *Journal of Mental Health Training, Education and Practice* **7** 89–94.

Cyhlarova E, Crepaz-Keay D, Reeves R, Morgan K, Lemmi V & Knapp M (2015) An evaluation of peer-led self-management training for people with severe psychiatric diagnoses. *Journal of Mental Health Training, Education and Practice* **10** (1) 3–13.

Lemmi V, Crepaz-Keay D, Cyhlarova E & Knapp M (2015) Peer-led self-management for people with severe mental disorders: an economic evaluation. *Journal of Mental Health Training, Education and Practice* **10** (1) 14–25.

Chapter 13: Speaking about ourselves: finding language to make sense of personal and collective identities

By Emma Perry

Introduction

This chapter draws on academic theory, specifically the philosophical approach known as 'post-structuralism', in order to inform thinking and discussion about language, identity and mental health. Post-structuralism arose during the mid 20th century as a response to the structuralist intellectual movement. Structuralist theorists took a scientific approach to language, claiming that human culture could be understood through the interpretation of linguistic signs and symbols (de Saussure, 1916). Their approach was criticised for its rigidity and failure to acknowledge the importance of different historical and cultural contexts. Proponents of post-structuralism take the position that reality is socially constructed in a variety of ways through language and that there are no grounds for privileging one explanation over another – arriving at a final truth is impossible; instead there are only multiple interpretations (Derrida, 1974; Kristeva, 1982).

Reading the work of post-structuralist theorists can often be confusing and frustrating. The ideas are complex and their writing can appear to be almost wilfully impenetrable and obtuse (Williams, 2005). Can post-structuralism be usefully applied outside of academia to our own lives, experiences and identities? I believe that it can, for the following reasons:

- It encourages us to develop a greater awareness of how language shapes understanding through the creation of 'discourses' or statements about a topic.

- It questions forms of knowledge that we might take for granted and assume as being self-evidently 'true'.

- It draws attention to the way in which language is used as a means of creating and maintaining power relations.

- It challenges mainstream perspectives that are presented as being 'universal' and creates space for marginalised voices to be heard.

- Specific post-structuralist theories, such as those discussed in this chapter, highlight the complexity and diversity of individual experiences and identities while also exploring the possibility of developing a group identity for the purposes of political campaigning.

Philosophical theories can be complex and may initially appear to be irrelevant when considering issues in the 'real world'. But they can also encourage us to question our beliefs and practices, and ultimately help us to challenge the status quo.

Language and identity

In 2013 the Royal College of Psychiatrists made a decision to replace the term 'service user' with 'patient' in their official documents. In an article for the Scottish Recovery Network, consultant psychiatrist David Christmas suggests that terms such as 'service user' and 'survivor', which emerged from the mental health activism of the 1960s and 70s, are no longer required because 'mental health activism has become much less radical and it has been able to establish a dialogue with a more conservative political landscape' (Christmas, 2013). He questions whether 'the language of radicalism' and 'a potent statement of self-identity' is still required, asserting that 'parity of esteem between mental and physical health becomes impossible unless we are all patients'.

Christmas views the term 'patient' as 'the collective term for a group of people who access a particular speciality of the NHS'. However, the language we use to describe ourselves and our mental health experience can also be the language of self-determination and agency. Language defines and shapes our understanding, but it is also fraught with complexity. The words we use help us to make sense of our own experiences and construct our own personal identities. These identities are not simply formed through our own discursive choices; they are also constructed in relation to power structures and the language others use to describe us (Althusser, 1971). Language has been used in many different social and historic contexts to pathologise and dominate people who have experienced mental distress (Foucault, 1967). For many people, receiving a psychiatric diagnosis and coming into contact with mental health services leads to stigma, discrimination, and a loss of agency and the right to self-representation (Chamberlin, 1978).

The decision of the Royal College of Psychiatrists to select the term 'patient' demonstrates the way in which language reflects underlying values and shapes attitudes through the promotion of certain discourses; in this case, through the understanding of mental health within a biomedical framework that views mental and emotional distress as 'psychiatric illness'. This decision makes sense within the specific context of the organisation, but it also contributes to the continued primacy of the medical model of 'mental illness', and the dominance of discourses that 'are still significantly based on a view of mental distress as a form of individualised pathology' (Beresford, 2009). Medicalised understandings of mental health can be restrictive due to their construction of people who experience mental distress within an essentialist binary of 'health' and 'illness'. Essentialism – the notion that a group of people share particular defining features – leads to stereotypical understandings of particular groups and their subsequent marginalisation and discrimination, for example on the basis of gender, ethnicity, sexuality or social class (Phillips, 2010).

Essentialism has been widely contested by feminist, postcolonial and queer theorists on the grounds that identity is culturally constructed rather than a biological given, and that people negotiate their identities in multiple, contradictory and dynamic ways (Butler, 1990; Nayak, 2001; Skeggs, 2004). In relation to mental health, this has led Schrader *et al* (2013) to describe a 'mad identity' as

'...not so much about a person's "intrinsic craziness", as the active and thoughtful positioning of the self with respect to dynamic social narratives regarding mental difference and diversity. To "identify" is to actively stake a personally and socially meaningful place in this complex assemblage of social, biological, and environmental forces; an assemblage that importantly includes (and actively grapples with) distress and psychological pain.' (p62)

As such, the mental health 'service user/survivor movement' encompasses a diverse array of individuals, local groups and national organisations. Members share common concerns and aim to support each other, promote the rights of people who have lived experience, and improve mental health services, policy and practice (Wallcraft *et al*, 2003). However, the movement is not a homogenous entity and there are a variety of perspectives on many issues, particularly relating to language. There is no agreement about terminology among 'service users' or 'survivors' and many terms are contested (Stickley, 2006; McLaughlin, 2009; Perry,

2014). Furthermore, words have different meanings within different groups and communities, and the ways in which we discuss the emotive topic of mental health is also affected by these diverse cultural contexts. This complexity is compounded when we think collectively about how to describe who we are and what constitutes our identities for the purposes of campaigning or political activism. To that end, this chapter explores the possibility of formulating a language in order to achieve a coherent group identity for the purposes of political campaigning, without negating or neglecting the inherent diversity and complexity of individual experiences, identities and the language used to describe them.

Preferred terms and personal identities

The National Survivor User Network (NSUN) is an organisation that is led by service users. It aims to connect people with experience of mental health issues and strengthen the service user voice in shaping policy and services at a local and national level. In order to inform organisational thinking with regard to terminology, NSUN wanted to discover what language its members preferred to use in relation to their own identities and mental health experience. A short online questionnaire was designed that aimed to find out which terms people identified with in the context of their own experiences, or of using mental health services. Respondents were asked to rank a list of terms (eg. 'service user', 'client', 'patient', 'person with a mental health problem') in order of preference from one to 13. They were then asked to explain why they identified with their chosen terms and were also invited to add their own preferred terms if they were not on the list. During 2013, 103 NSUN members completed the survey and results showed that the most popular term was 'person with direct or lived experience of mental distress'. However, a number of people struggled to rank their preferences numerically, which highlighted the problematic nature of the task and the multiple and complex nature of identities (see Perry, 2014 for further analysis). These complexities were also reflected within the qualitative responses, which frequently questioned the apparently fixed and stable nature of identity.

The following key themes were identified through analysis of the qualitative responses:

- **The rigid and restrictive nature of identity markers**
  A number of respondents questioned or rejected terms because they did not accurately or completely capture the complexity of people's lived experiences.

- ### The importance of context and setting
  Respondents challenged the fixed nature of identity markers by highlighting the importance of context. Many constructed their own identities as inherently flexible and selected terms depending upon emotional experience, setting or 'requirement' when engaging with mental health services.

- ### The need for identity markers that do not perpetuate stigma and discrimination
  There was a rejection of identity markers and labels that were seen to perpetuate discrimination. Although people related to terms very differently depending on how they made sense of their own experiences and how they positioned themselves in relation to the medical model, all were united in a desire to challenge stigma and discrimination and to be treated equally.

- ### Being respected and valued as a person
  Related to the need to move away from restrictive labels and identity markers was an emphasis on the importance of recognising and valuing each person. Many of the preferred terms in the survey began with the words 'person with…'. One respondent explained, 'I rate highest those terms which remind the listener (esp. professionals) that I am a person just like them'.

- ### Focus on lived experience
  Respondents positioned themselves in different ways with regard to understandings of 'illness', but all emphasised the lived experiential aspects of identity.

- ### Value of expertise and emphasis on empowerment
  Respondents were more likely to identify with terms that promoted positive choices, emphasised the skills and 'expertise' gained through lived experiences, and focused on active empowerment.

The themes and values to emerge from the data highlighted that the terms people identified with were often based on how they helped to make sense of their own lived experiences. The findings also demonstrated that respondents were not keen to attach themselves to a singular identity that defined their experience of mental distress. Instead, people constructed and negotiated their personal identities in unique and complex ways, in different settings. Individual experiences also inform membership of groups, as people can find value and purpose in working together with others who share their experiences and concerns, and this may also intersect with other parts of their identity.

Although progress is being made within mental health policy and practice with regard to user involvement and co-production (Faulkner, 2014) the dominant discourse of mental health continues to be biomedical and led by professionals. This discourse is evidenced in the DSM-5 debates (Decker, 2013; Levine, 2013), the recent findings of Mental Health Minimum Datasets (HSCIC, 2013), CQC findings on involuntary admissions (CQC, 2014) and Community Treatment Orders (Lawton-Smith, 2010). It therefore remains important to find a radical collective language that enables campaigning, but that is mindful of heterogeneity. One possibility is by drawing on the concept of 'strategic essentialism'.

Theorising collective identities for political purposes

'Strategic essentialism' was introduced by the postcolonial theorist Gayatri Chakravorty Spivak (1987) in relation to the Subaltern Studies Group, which aimed to rethink the history of India by deconstructing the dominant imperialist version and reviving the 'subaltern consciousness' in order to develop a postcolonial India. Spivak defines strategic essentialism as the 'strategic use of positivist essentialism in a scrupulously political interest' (p281). It invokes the idea of an essentialist category while simultaneously critiquing it and recognising diversity among members of the group. Hall (2013) has described this 'anti-identity identity politics' in the following manner:

> 'We have strength when we create a "we" out of the isolation and divide-and-conquer of oppression. So I can speak for shared experience, to some degree, as long as I also create that welcome space for diversity that negates identity for a moment.'

As such, it can enable minority groups or political formations to promote a collective identity in a standardised and simplified way in order to engage with a dominant culture, challenge power structures and achieve specific political objectives. This requires a shared language, but this temporary essentialisation is aware of the shifting nature of context and allows and encourages group members to engage in discussions and debates about ongoing differences.

Strategic essentialism has been a controversial concept however, and theorists such as Judith Butler (1990) have expressed concern with regard to the notion of asserting a 'false' essence or identity that it is possible to control or manipulate. She also draws attention to the problem of representation and who is speaking on behalf of whom. Similarly, Fuss (1990) states that 'the radicality or conservatism of essentialism depends, to a significant degree, on who is utilizing it, how it is deployed, and where its effects are concentrated' (p20). Thus, it is possible for 'strategic essentialism' to continue to create power hierarchies and marginalise others. For example, a mental health service user who is white, heterosexual, male and middle class may have more access and opportunity to speak than others within a group who have more marginalised social identities.

Spivak herself later distanced herself from the phrase 'strategic essentialism', although not the concept itself, which she still believed to be helpful (Danius *et al*, 1993). She felt that people had misused the concept and ignored and neglected the 'strategic' element. She explained that in many cases 'strategic essentialism' had lapsed into uncritical, reductive and marginalising essentialist thought. Consequently, she called for a greater understanding of the situational specificity of strategy and greater awareness for determining when essentialising strategies had become 'traps' rather than creating the intended strategic and necessary positive effects.

Other concepts have also been considered in order to address the question of whether it may be possible to form a collective identity for political purposes while avoiding essentialism. For example, Becky Francis (2012) has used insights from the Russian linguist and cultural theorist Mikhail Bakhtin (1981) in order to theorise gender. Her work explores alternative conceptualisations of gender that avoid essentialism, while acknowledging the impact of social structures and the need to formulate a language to mobilise a collective identity. Although her work focuses on the construction of social identities in educational contexts, the linguistic concepts she draws on (that of Bakhtin's 'monoglossia' and 'heteroglossia') could be usefully applied to a mental health context.

According to Bakhtin, dominant forms of language – 'monoglossia' – reflect and construct the values and interests of dominant social groups. They take the appearance of being natural, fixed, stable and unifying. Dominant monoglossic accounts position themselves as 'true'. However, language operating at a more individualised, personal level is inherently diverse, dynamic and evolving. Bakhtin refers to this as 'heteroglossia'. For example, dominant psychiatric discourses, which focus on biomedical understandings of mental 'health' and 'illness', are monoglossic in nature. But although there may appear to be linguistic stability at a monoglossic level, individual utterances are in fact characterised by contradiction and resistance. At a heteroglossic level, individuals are able to challenge, subvert and resist dominant discourses and language. Francis (2012) therefore argues that it is possible to resist essentialism and engage with dominant monoglossic discourses if there is also an ongoing recognition of the complex, nuanced, heteroglossic ways in which personal identities are constructed.

Practical application

This theoretical discussion of language and identity raises the question of how these concepts and ideas can inform practice within local service user/survivor groups and statutory organisations. With regard to any group or service, the development process regarding relationships and language will vary. Practically, when forming new groups or non-statutory organisations, consideration of the following may aid the development of a self-defined culture:

■ Focused meetings and consultations that develop terms of reference or memorandums of understanding can create a forum for open discussion about identity and language. They can provide an opportunity to negotiate shared terms and approaches while acknowledging difference and diversity. Any documents produced should be used as a starting point and regularly referred back to.

■ Group agreements in meetings usually include items such as confidentiality, respect and appropriate use of language. This can be explored further within any group – what do terms mean to people personally?

■ Style guides and ethical policies can be useful documents that also include the agreed use of terminology and language. Once again, these documents should be regularly reviewed and seen as dynamic rather than fixed.

■ Training and leadership programmes can incorporate open discussions around identity and language.

■ Groups can conduct regular polling and surveys to gain a greater understanding of group members' thoughts about language use.

■ Work should be linked across health and social care groups. Language use in shared contexts, such as pan-disability groups, should be considered.

Statutory organisations and institutions could consider the following:

■ The involvement of people who use services at all levels of an organisation can and does change the use of 'acceptable' language. The depersonalisation of people and their circumstances happens less often when they are present.

■ Strategies and policies can all include value statements and be supported by training and staff supervision that reflects the policies and guidance.

■ Working with people and organisations to regularly reflect on and review approaches and policies that impact on language and staff approach.

■ Large organisations and institutions can draw on research led by service users and survivors to inform their policies and approaches to language.

Conclusion

The 'language of radicalism' continues to be necessary in order to engage with and challenge dominant medicalised discourses. Whether service user-led groups and mental health organisations choose to draw on 'strategic essentialism' or alternative concepts in order to grapple with these ideas, they will need to take into consideration the diversity of membership and intersecting contexts of experiences that inform people's identities and use of language. These understandings will also need to be connected to the organisation's values, role and purpose. It is important to find a collective language in order to challenge dominant discourses, but this need not be divisive or restrictive. A focus on shared values and an awareness of heterogeneity can allow for difference, whether we refer to ourselves as 'survivors', 'service users', 'patients' or 'people with lived experience'.

References

Althusser L (1971) Ideology and ideological state apparatuses. In: L Althusser (Ed) *Lenin and Philosophy and other Essays*. New York: Monthly Review Press.

Bahktin M (1981) *The Dialogic Imagination: Four essays*. M Holquist (Ed) (trans. C Emerson and M Holquist). Austin, TX and London: University of Texas Press.

Beresford P (2009) Developing a social model of madness and distress to underpin survivor research. In: A Sweeney, P Beresford, A Faulkner, M Nettle and D Rose (Eds) *This is Survivor Research* (pp44–52). Ross-on-Wye: PCCS Books.

Butler J (1990) *Gender Trouble*. Abingdon: Routledge.

Care Quality Commission (2014) *Monitoring the Mental Health Act in 2012/13* [online]. Available at: http://www.cqc.org.uk/sites/default/files/documents/cqc_mentalhealth_2012_13_07_update.pdf (accessed February 2015).

Chamberlin J (1978) *On Our Own: Patient-controlled alternatives to the mental health system*. New York: Haworth Press.

Christmas D (2013) *Should Patients be Patients?* [online]. Available at: http://www.scottishrecovery.net/Latest-News/should-patients-be-patients.html (accessed February 2015).

Danius S, Jonsson S & Spivak GC (1993) An interview with Gayatri Chakravorty Spivak. *Boundary 2* **20** (2) 24–50.

Decker HS (2013) *Why the Fuss Over the DSM-5, When Did the DSM Start to Matter, & For How Long Will it Continue to?* [online]. Available at: https://www.madinamerica.com/2013/06/why-the-fuss-over-the-dsm-5-when-did-it-start-to-matter-and-how-much-longer-will-it/ (accessed February 2015).

Derrida J (1974) *Of Grammatology* (trans. GC Spivak). Baltimore, MD: Johns Hopkins University Press.

de Saussure F (1916) *Course in General Linguistics*. USA: Open Court.

Faulkner A (2015) *National Involvement Partnership 4PI Standards for Involvement* [online]. London: NSUN. Available at: www.nsun.org.uk/about-us/our-work/national-involvement-partnership (accessed April 2015).

Foucault M (1967) *Madness and Civilization: A history of insanity in the age of reason* (trans. R. Howard). London and New York: Routledge.

Francis B (2012) Gender monoglossia, gender heteroglossia: the potential of Bakhtin's work for re-conceptualising gender. *Journal of Gender Studies* **21** (1) 1–16.

Fuss D (1990) *Essentially Speaking: Feminism, nature and difference*. London: Routledge.

Hall W (2013) *Will Hall on the Anti-identity Identity Politics of Madness* [online]. Available at: http://malingeringnormal.wordpress.com/2013/12/09/will-hall-on-the-anti-identity-identity-politics-of-madness/ (accessed February 2015).

Health and Social Care Information Centre (2013) *Mental Health Bulletin: Annual report from MHMDS returns – England 2012/13* [online]. Available at: http://www.hscic.gov.uk/catalogue/PUB12745/mhb-1213-ann-rep.pdf (accessed February 2015).

Kristeva J (1982) *The Powers of Horror*. New York: Columbia University Press.

Lawton-Smith S (2010) *Supervised Community Treatment* [online]. London: Mental Health Alliance. Available at: http://www.mentalhealthalliance.org.uk/resources/SCT_briefing_paper.pdf (accessed February 2015).

Levine B (2013) *Rejuvenating Abolitionism of Psychiatric Labels – Even Some Establishment Psychiatrists Embarrassed by New DSM-5* [online]. Available at: https://www.madinamerica.com/2013/02/rejuvenating-abolitionism-of-psychiatric-labels-even-some-establishment-psychiatrists-embarrassed-by-new-dsm-5/ (accessed February 2015).

McLaughlin H (2009) What's in a name: 'client', 'patient', 'customer', 'consumer', 'expert by experience', 'service user' – what's next? *British Journal of Social Work* **19** (6) 1101–1117.

Nayak A (2001) 'Ice white and ordinary': new perspectives on ethnicity, gender, and youth cultural identities. In: B Francis and C Skelton (Eds) *Investigating Gender: Contemporary perspectives in education*. Berkshire: Open University Press.

Perry E (2014) *The Language of Mental Wellbeing*, London: NSUN, National Involvement Partnership [online]. Available at: http://www.nsun.org.uk/assets/downloadableFiles/4Pi-LANGUAGEOFMENTALWELLBEING.V42.pdf (accessed April 2015).

Phillips A (2010) What's wrong with essentialism? *Distinktion: Scandinavian journal of social theory* **11** (1) 47–60.

Schrader S, Jones N & Shatell M (2013) Mad pride: reflections on sociopolitical identity and mental diversity in the context of culturally competent psychiatric care. *Issues in Mental Health Nursing* **34** 62–64.

Skeggs B (2004) *Class, Self, Culture*. London: Routledge.

Spivak GC (1987) *In Other Worlds: Essays in cultural politics*. Abingdon: Routledge.

Stickley T (2006) Should service user involvement be consigned to history? A critical realist perspective. *Journal of Psychiatric and Mental Health Nursing* **13** (5) 570–577.

Wallcraft J, Read J & Sweeney A (2003) *On Our Own Terms*. London: Sainsbury Centre for Mental Health.

Williams J (2005) *Understanding Poststructuralism*. London: Routledge.

Chapter 14: Service user involvement and peer support: yesterday, today and tomorrow

By Anne Beales

Introduction

When Together's Service User Involvement Directorate (SUID) was first formed in 2004, the service user movement already existed as a radical voice made up of individual leaders (activists) and small local groups of people supporting each other through mental distress. Over time, we began sharing what worked for us, and simultaneously worked with the establishment[12] to reform what they offered us. With few resources other than commitment, experience and goodwill, we remained outside and separate from the establishment, sometimes becoming tiny 'providers' of research, training, consultancy and peer support. The impact of our campaigning, lobbying and working as partners has been groundbreaking and the most significant force in the reform (transformation) agenda.

Since its inception, the SUID has been committed to supporting the building of a national infrastructure for service user led initiatives. As traditional hierarchical leadership often mirrors the negative experiences people face within the establishment, the structure that developed for this purpose was, in contrast, a network that linked to and supported local initiatives. Particular attention was paid to ensuring people from minority communities, who were over-represented in the most restrictive services, were included and given space to be heard.

---

12 When I refer to the 'establishment', I simply mean the official mental health system, comprising professionals, policy makers and politicians who determine how we (people who experience mental distress) are perceived and treated, for better or for worse.

In March 2005, in partnership with the Mental Health Foundation, Together hosted a national conference for service users and service user groups, which led to a mandate for Together to establish a network of service user groups that could express a collective perspective. Funding was secured and the result was the National Survivor User Network (NSUN), hosted by Together until it developed sufficiently to establish its own identity as an independent charity.

NSUN developed training for 'champions' who were individuals wanting to develop service user led networks in their local areas. Some of the training was accredited by universities and overall it had an overwhelmingly positive reception from participants. A model of support where training is followed by the offer of volunteering was not new, but the fact it was led by small service user led groups across England, many of whom were formed for that very purpose, was a huge step forward. Service user groups, which struggled so hard to survive, undertook and delivered all this while working within the establishment on the reform and transformation agenda. (For more information, see www.nsun.org.uk/about-us/our-reports-and-publications-we-refer-to-in-our-work)

When Together established its SUID in 2004, we set out to reflect what was working in service user led groups around England, by creating local and national forums that offered the opportunity to influence the organisation at every level, while providing a way for people to reacquaint themselves with their skills, learn new ones and regain purpose in their everyday lives. Crucially, the process was led by people with experience of using mental health services. This approach is represented in Figure 14.1.

This well-being approach to involving people has the dual outcome of providing both peer support and training, and can be adapted for delivery in a range of settings, such as secure services and prisons. It is adaptable enough to enable current or new providers to deliver it, providing service users lead on the implementation.

Together used this model (which reflected what local service user led groups offered) across the whole organisation to:

■ increase awareness and understanding of well-being and how to support it from the service user perspective

■ enable self-management, self-directed support and development of peer support and social inclusion

■ involve service users at all levels, ensuring that lived experience provided influence and insight into developments

- act as a support for organisational change (eg. development of the Your Way model of community support[13])

- be a practical impetus to make best use of current tools and expertise (eg. care plans)

- promote employment and education opportunities

- enable support for people from marginalised and minority groups in a self-directed way.

Figure 14.1

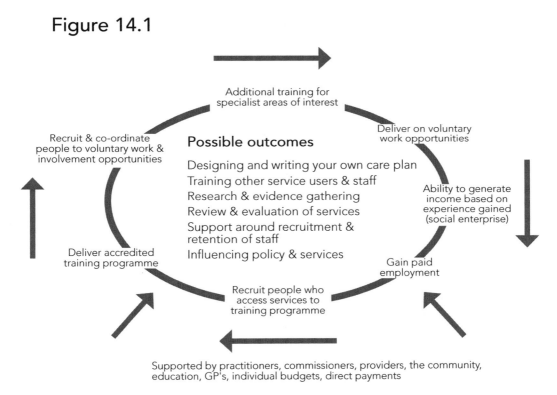

Additional training for specialist areas of interest

Deliver on voluntary work opportunities

Recruit & co-ordinate people to voluntary work & involvement opportunities

Possible outcomes

Designing and writing your own care plan
Training other service users & staff
Research & evidence gathering
Review & evaluation of services
Support around recruitment & retention of staff
Influencing policy & services

Ability to generate income based on experience gained (social enterprise)

Deliver accredited training programme

Gain paid employment

Recruit people who access services to training programme

Supported by practitioners, commissioners, providers, the community, education, GP's, individual budgets, direct payments

(Beales & Platts, 2008)

From involvement to peer support

If the primary purpose of involvement is to support people through distress, then we must take a lead from those who have experienced that distress, no matter if this 'instinctive' approach doesn't fit a scientific model. Occasionally, the impact

13 For more information, see www.together-uk.org/our-mental-health-services/your-way

of this mutual support among peers will influence the practice of professionals; where we are listened to and understood, we can have a positive impact on providers and regulators (even if rarely at policy level). Some service user led groups, however, have no interest in reforming the establishment and focus instead on delivering peer support with the tiniest of grants from commissioners. Others feel that to leave their peers working in isolation within the establishment is irresponsible, and so reach inwards to offer training, even supervision and, exceptionally, the direct provision of peer-led peer support[14].

As people who access services within Together and speak up via the SUID, our vision for the future is one where we are self-managing, with appropriate support that we ourselves design, governing ourselves individually and as a movement (for an example of self-management and peer support in action, see Chapter 12). The logical consequence of this is that stigma, prejudice and ignorance are reduced. We feel compelled to achieve this so our past struggles lead to a better future.

Peer support in practice

One of the major successes of service user led groups is the solidarity they provide. We understand that some people's distress is characterised by loneliness, isolation and stigma. Renewed hope and confidence has to be discovered by each of us – it cannot be given to us. Service user led groups can give people the maximum opportunity to make this discovery.

Service user leadership in peer support

As time passes, our knowledge and skills – which are based on our experience – are becoming an ever-growing resource for others, which is in turn translated into reforms at all levels. We continue to develop, innovate, explain and articulate what works for us within and outside of the establishment. We are setting standards for involvement, protecting our role in history, and still working away at overcoming barriers to influencing policy in a meaningful way, while also developing an infrastructure to talk to each other and be heard by others[15].

The language of service user involvement came comparatively late in our history (for a more detailed discussion of language, see Chapter 13). The movement began in opposition to the medicalisation of our distress, and our demands echoed those of previous human rights struggles. We were overtly political, a position some

---

14 For more information, see www.peerworker.sgul.ac.uk/peer-worker-research-briefing-paper.pdf

15 For more information, see www.nsun.org.uk/assets/downloadableFiles/4pi.-ni-standards-for-web2.pdf

of us are finding ourselves compelled to adopt once again internationally and at home as medicalisation persists within the establishment[16].

Where service user led initiatives grew and developed organically in the community, they tended to be developed in isolation using a variety of activities and language, with varying degrees of quality and effectiveness.

Challenges facing peer support

There are a number of challenges facing peer support groups across the country. Two of these challenges are highlighted below.

Challenge 1: resources

Service user led groups rely on being able to generate income in order to survive, let alone flourish. Funding is so hard to come by that it can feel as if money goes only towards finding more money, and this is especially true when funding an infrastructure rather than frontline services. The Peer2Peer Network is one such example of this. This network of service user led groups and individuals is still alive against all the odds, and in transition from being hosted by Together to being hosted (funding permitting) by NSUN[17].

The Peer2Peer Network is supported by organisations such as St George's London University, which is evaluating the effectiveness of such networks, where people can share ideas and good practice around peer support and offer advice. While some service user led initiatives remain informal, unpaid and very separate from other provision in mental health, others have become 'micro-providers' reliant on income via contracts to pay staff such as peer supporters, often on a sessional basis. Many such workers still rely on the benefits system, so have to work within the boundaries that this demands. This leads us to the question of whether such service user groups are part of a social movement, or indeed the voluntary sector of tomorrow? Taking the Queen's shilling from commissioners could put the provision of independent peer support at risk, let alone campaigning and challenging. Becoming formal 'providers' with terms and conditions, targets and outcomes, can tie up the expertise and energy of small service user led groups. The tendering process is a discipline in itself, meaning that the development of peer support sometimes has to happen 'under the radar'. Some service user led groups remain unaware that what they do is what some would call peer support – they simply get on with doing what works for them without any contact from professionals.

16 For more information, see www.interrelate.info

17 For more information, see www.nsun.org.uk/about-us/our-work/peer2peer/

Challenge 2: relationship with statutory services and the risk of co-option

Sadly, some service user led groups are kept at a distance by the establishment providers offering something they call peer support, but which is at best a means of work creation for people who have used services. Paid peer supporters are substituted (sometimes in isolation) into existing teams, with pay inevitably being at the lower end of the scale. Their lived experience of mental distress plays no role. Where peer supporters are simply making up staff numbers in this way, they have to be insured and adhere to the same policies and procedures as staff. We have heard of cases where peer supporters have been required to learn 'control and restraint techniques', or to notify professionals of instances of non-compliance with medication. Rather than leading to self-management, their practice becomes a reflection of the practice of those surrounding them[18].

Some have even suggested that peer supporters should be seen as a 'third' profession alongside nursing and social work, an idea supported by some academics and providers. However, this is a serious misinterpretation of the essence of peer support. The strength of peer support lies in mutuality. This is what distinguishes us from mental health professionals. As peers we can discuss the abuse, disadvantage and isolation we have experienced. We are experts in what works for us and can pass this expertise on. If we then want to become a professional in the mental health field, we can apply to do so on our merits, free from discrimination.

When statutory or large voluntary sector organisations attempt to mimic what service user led groups are practising, we all too often see things get lost in translation. SUID has for 10 years consistently promoted the voice of people who use services, and the importance of hearing what works for them. The aim of achieving self-management (via peer support) is one that poses some interesting conundrums. To sustain service user leadership within Together's peer support provision, SUID supports a number of paid peer support co-ordinators to deliver training and implement peer support by matching and developing the supporters with the supported. If we do not have a peer support co-ordinator in an area, we don't train peer supporters, as an infrastructure is essential to their well-being. Some of our peer supporters are volunteers who work for a time alongside people who are distressed, as part of a transition they themselves are making towards recovery. They are co-ordinated, trained and supported with the aim of demonstrating and modelling self-management in action[19].

---

18 For more information, see www.together-uk.org/about-us/peer-support/

19 For more information, see www.together-uk.org/wp-content/uploads/downloads/2014/06/Service-User-Involvement-briefing.pdf

Next steps

All those years ago, we insisted we should not be harmed by getting involved and speaking up. Now we have developed service user leadership, which for us and those who understand, means using our experience of what works to guide positive change. We have developed our own style of non-hierarchical leadership by 'networking' to lead ourselves in our ambitions and aspirations.

The future then must be about respecting and valuing the leadership role of people who use services in the transformation and reform agenda, while also developing as a collective with the purpose of supporting each other through distress. Our success depends on true service user leadership and partnerships where service users truly work alongside those designing and delivering mental health support. It also depends on a certain degree of 'intelligent disinvestment' in the establishment and a shift instead towards investing in service user led groups to deliver their own solutions.

The future must also be about passing on our learning to the wider healthcare sector[20]. We must find the energy to articulate what works for us when, as people who access the mental health system, our physical health is at risk and we need physical medical attention. And we must share this expertise with those who so often become depressed and distressed as they face terminal or life-changing physical illness. We must guard against potentially disempowering initiatives where professionals discharge themselves of their duty to involve people by undertaking misguided 'engagement' practices such as patient satisfaction surveys. We must ensure that the future collective voice of service users includes those in forensic services, who have experience of what works as some of the most troubled people. And we must negotiate the benefits and pitfalls of either remaining an isolated movement made up of 'micro-providers' or working with the establishment to increase investment in the approaches we ourselves design and promote.

What is clear is that the status quo has not met – and does not meet – our needs in the way we want. As long as the emphasis is on being 'symptom free with medication' rather than tackling the abuse, stigma and poverty routinely experienced by people with mental health problems, our goal of 'getting well' will continue to elude us. So long as the status quo is maintained by power structures, our society will continue to 'madden' us, medicalise us, impose systems that we've had no hand in creating.

However, if we are supported to understand where our experience of distress comes from and what perpetuates that distress, to explain our human need and what

20 For more information, see www.nationalvoices.org.uk/nv-member-news

works for us, we can lead the way in defining provision, quality, cost, and finally policy. In short, as with resolving much of the world's human need and suffering, the answers are political. We hear frequently of 'paradigm shifts', 'parity of esteem' (for a detailed discussion on parity of esteem, see Chapter 6), 'offering choice', 'ease of access' (decreased waiting times) and 'prioritising prevention'. In many ways, the next struggle is less about opposition and more about addressing the reality of implementing these policies and ideals. As those who designed the new paradigm, who pushed for it to benefit ourselves and others, we must remain the guardians of the implementation of change. Most importantly, we must continue to push for the appropriate resources for implementation.

Service user experience and leadership must continue to gain purchase at every level of service provision. If even modest investment was made in an infrastructure of service user led initiatives such as peer support and mechanisms for sharing learning about what works for us, the change would be vast. This can and should happen beyond mental health settings too, as is already often the case with service user led initiatives. Services that are solidly based on hearing and acting on the views of those who have solutions based on experience will always succeed, regardless of context or setting.

What service user leadership offers is a new way of life. It is the force for social change in our very own communities that we must remain part of in spite of our distress; indeed, because of our distress. The fight for good mental health and well-being is inextricably linked to ending the prejudice and disadvantage that still exists in our communities. In other words, the next changes and challenges will necessarily be linked to social justice and implementing the human rights agenda.

References

Beales A & Platz G (2008) Working in partnership. In: T Stickley and T Bassett (Eds) *Learning About Mental Health Practice*. Chichester: John Wiley & Sons.

Chapter 15: Lessons from Lille

By David Crepaz-Keay, Eva Cyhlarova, Nicolas Daumerie and Massimo Marsili

Context

Policy

Many people believe that mental health services in the UK have become unsustainable in their current form. Current services cost too much and deliver too little. Crises happen because people cannot get the support they need when they need it. Sometimes this is due to people being stuck in expensive healthcare settings because they cannot get the social care they need, sometimes people end up in the criminal justice system because they cannot get the mental health care they need. These problems have been identified for years and solutions have been sought from far and wide.

However, there is a potential solution under our noses, in Lille, France, 90 minutes away by train. This chapter is based on information sharing between the authors and colleagues over many years of European collaboration and recent study visits involving more detailed examination of the day-to-day practicalities with an eye to what may work in a UK setting.

History

Although this chapter will concentrate on the services of East Lille, the philosophy underpinning these services was first developed and applied in Italy by Franco Basaglia, firstly in Gorizia (1961–69) and subsequently in Trieste (1971–79). This section draws on *Psychiatry Inside Out: Selected writings of Franco Basaglia* (Scheper-Hughes & Lovell, 1987).

Basaglia qualified as a psychiatrist and began to practise just after the Second World War, and he was greatly influenced by the way psychiatry was co-opted by the Nazis. During the war, hundreds of thousands of people with a psychiatric diagnosis were either killed or sterilised as part of a process of genocide under the Nazi regime. This was made easier by the notion that mental illness was a symptom of biochemical flaws transmitted across generations by genes and therefore removable from the population. (A discussion of the actual impact of the removal of at least three-quarters of all people with a diagnosis of schizophrenia from the German population – which had no apparent long-term effect on the subsequent incidence of schizophrenia – can be found in Torrey & Yolken, 2009.)

In order to develop a system of support that could not be misappropriated for such malign purposes, and one which moved away from a biochemical and genetic deficit model, Basaglia set out to dismantle the prevailing locked institutional approach and replace it with what we would now recognise as the social model of disability.

Basaglia's achievements in Gorizia had two key components: an open ward policy that included employing patients in paid roles across the hospital, and daily meetings between patients and staff (and indeed anyone from the local population who wished to attend). Between them, these transformations provided the means and opportunities for patients to develop and articulate their own concerns and share them with staff and the broader community. This also started a shift of thinking from the individual as the source of the problem and the institution as the source of the solution towards a collective view of both problem and solution, which was subsequently developed and delivered in Trieste and lives on in Lille.

The work of Franco Basaglia and colleagues in Trieste took the philosophy much further and dismantled an existing hospital to provide a completely different framework for understanding and supporting the then 1,200 patients and their successors. This transformation was underpinned by a rights-based approach in which patients were granted a new legal status as *ospiti* (guests) and their full civil rights were restored. The goal was more than just dismantling an institution – it was about creating a whole and supportive community. This meant that, alongside reconnecting patients with the community, it required the even greater challenge of reconnecting the community with the psychiatric patients the community had institutionalised.

Support for the former patients was provided by using small apartments, initially within the existing hospital grounds but subsequently in the wider community. Workers' co-operatives were established to give *ospiti* constructive roles and wages, and the support given to people was socially orientated, provided by peers and members of the community as well as by professionals. All medication and psychotherapy became voluntary.

Basaglia believed it was essential to encourage the broader community to connect with and embrace the *ospiti*, and he chose art and culture as the tools for the task.

This was not art as therapy, rather it was creating a new shared culture for the community as a whole, with the process of creation being initially led by the *ospiti*.

These are the foundations upon which the transformation of the services in East Lille were based.

About East Lille

The area covered by the psychiatric services of East Lille comprises six towns with the total population of 86,000 (comparable to Ashford, Kent, or about one-third of the population of Hackney or Tower Hamlets). As it is close to the Nord-Pas-de-Calais region, about 4.2% of the population is of foreign origin. Compared to the national average in France, the city has significantly more disadvantage. For example, it has the shortest life expectancy in France (79.6 years) and a high death rate (eg. the highest rate of tobacco or alcohol related deaths at 14.1 per 10,000 population aged 40 to 64 years). It also performs particularly badly in terms of poverty and employment rates (15.6% unemployment, compared to the 'national average' of 11.1%), and has an under-resourced health system (Roelandt *et al*, 2014).

What Lille has achieved

Before its transformation in 1975, East Lille was served by a large psychiatric hospital with 300 patients which consumed 98% of the mental health budget. Few community services existed and there was no physical, social or cultural connection between the institution and the broader community.

Built on the foundation of Franco Basaglia's approach, the services in East Lille have developed what they consider to be a community response to a community challenge. This approach has involved completely changing the ways in which the services are provided. Although no individual component is completely new, or even particularly complicated, the overall impact has been remarkable. The average stay in hospital has been reduced from 213 days to 6.5 while the number of people receiving care and support from the service has risen from 589 to 2,572. A more detailed analysis of changes in service use is provided in table 15.1 on p160.

Key service resources

Community solutions to community challenges

The underpinning philosophy that really marks the services in East Lille as different from UK services is that the problems are whole community challenges

Table 15.1: Changing patterns of care				
For 86,000 inhabitants	1971	2002	2010	2012
No. of people receiving care	589	1,677	2,572	2,798
Community care (no. of interventions)	0	23,478	48,315	61,058
Admission to hospital/acute beds	145	444	360	301
No. of hospital beds available	209	26	12	10
Compulsory admissions	145 (100%)	99 (22%)	87 (24%)	84 (28%)
Mean length of stay (in days)	213	14.5	6.5	7.5
No. of people admitted to host families		87	63	64
No. of people admitted to homecare treatment			234	300

(Adapted from Roelandt *et al*, 2014)

that require whole community solutions, rather than a number of ill individuals who need treatments in community settings.

In order to make this transition, there has been significant investment in time and resources into ensuring community involvement. This has been a long-term, focused endeavour. Anti-discrimination and stigma work with a purpose in mind.

Host families

Therapeutic host families are used in Lille as an alternative to hospitalisation for people in an acute situation. The host families form an integral part of the services, and are paid for their care and support. Currently, 12 places are available, and the average length of stay is 21 days. Support is provided by home visits of the social and medical teams in a similar way to when people are in hospital (eg. treatment, links to activities). Therapeutic activities are offered in the town's consultation and activity centres.

High intensity support in a community setting

There is a small crisis house that allows people to stay for up to eight days. The high intensity support includes a multidisciplinary team but also involves GPs, pharmacists, family and friends so that the care is developed by everyone involved in the delivery, not by mental health professionals in isolation.

Housing

Associative flats are part of the public housing in Lille and are allocated by a committee of representatives of Intermunicipalities Council for Health, Mental Health and Citizenship, public housing offices, social landlords, users, carers etc. The flats are usually shared by two or three people and a student. Intermunicipalities Council for Health, Mental Health and Citizenship provides the deposit and the tenants cover the rent and bills. At present, 57 flats are being used by 95 people. The mobile teams are in charge of medical, social and educational support, and the tenants have regular consultations with a psychiatrist and a nurse, apart from other therapeutic activities. The mobile teams are available 24 hours a day, seven days a week (Roelandt *et al*, 2014).

An associative and therapeutic residence (named 'Andre Breton') is also part of the public housing system and provides an alternative to segregation of people with severe problems in specialised homes. It has six sheltered flats and one large flat for six tenants with severe problems. The residence is staffed 24/7 by care assistants, health education assistants etc.

Housing to avoid long-term hospitalisation

Residence 'Ambroise Pare' is part of a social programme with low rent accommodation in Lille, and includes four flats of various sizes, for users/tenants and students to share.

Residence 'Samuel Beckett' is for people coming out of long-term hospital stays, as a first step to a new service. It has a flat for a host family, and another five-room flat used as a transition place for people going on to another type of accommodation (eg. sheltered or social housing). A nurse is in charge of the treatment, and the educational team visits in the evenings and at weekends, and assesses people's self-sufficiency and their ability to live alone etc (Roelandt *et al*, 2014).

Cultural approaches

Artistic creativity is seen as allowing equality, no matter if people are users or artists. This is not seen as art therapy (cure through art), but rather as a 'non-stigmatisation' partnership with artists. The current artistic activities have evolved from the old hospital and the hospital/culture partnership for 'rehabilitation'. Now all the cultural structures of the city take part in these activities.

For the last year there has been a full-time post of an arts professor. Art groups are led by artists and supervised by nurses. Some groups are organised by art institutions, such as dance schools, for example, or art schools (Roelandt *et al*, 2014).

Service practice

When you see the service in action there are a number of ways in which the processes are markedly different from what we are used to. A number in particular seem to underpin the behaviours of services and staff that make the difference between success and failure on a day-to-day basis.

Art, culture and community inclusion is at the heart of all practice. The aim is to maintain complete integration with the broader community even during crisis. Art and culture underpin the service not as therapy, but as a mechanism for social inclusion.

Daily conference calls

At the beginning of every day the entire team for East Lille meet together either physically or through a conference call. The most pressing issues are discussed and, if immediate actions are required, then the necessary people will leave the meeting to attend to the matters at once. As everyone is present, it is possible to quickly decide who the best person to take responsibility is, and if they need input from a different professional then they can get it during the meeting or arrange a one-to-one to occur at an appropriate time.

The meetings are not hierarchical, but they are disciplined. If something needs doing it gets done, but if it can wait it gets left. As the meetings are daily, things that are not discussed on the day can still be addressed within days rather than weeks or months.

The risk spreadsheet and live information

In order to support these daily meetings, and in particular to help prioritise discussions, the team maintains a single spreadsheet identifying everyone currently in contact with any of its services, and the primary team in charge of the person's care. Every service user is colour coded for risk so that it is easy to ascertain where the level or type of support needs to be adjusted.

All services are open and no one is compelled to accept treatment

There is a new ward in the central hospital in Lille which takes patients, but it would not be recognised as a hospital by those of us familiar with UK psychiatric hospitals. The low numbers of patients combined with the ward's open nature mean there is a calm atmosphere. The artistic and cultural nature of the community is also apparent in the hospital building and the focus of activities. There are many treatments that we would more readily associate with a spa or retreat than a psychiatric hospital, including steam rooms and hydrotherapy. The emphasis is on physical and mental well-being, not symptoms and illness.

Genuinely mobile teams with rapid response rates and fast referrals

One of the keys to removing reliance on hospital admissions is enabling people to get help quickly when they need it. There are multiple routes to access services, including GPs, general hospitals and twice-weekly clinics for non-urgent referrals. Nurses and psychiatrists are available 24 hours a day and will respond with a home visit at any time if it is considered necessary.

Could it work here?

Some substantial blocks remain

Nothing that is done in Lille is magic, but neither is it straightforward. It is worth noting that even in France this approach has not been wholly replicated. It is not a model that would be easy to adopt in its entirety in England, though Wales and Scotland may find it easier.

Illness focused, bed obsessed

The biggest single block to the paradigm shift required is our stubborn focus on an illness/treatment approach. Our services are designed to deliver treatments. This combined with a fixation on the hospital bed as a *sine qua non* of any service makes it difficult for people to imagine services as different as those in Lille. However it is dressed up, this illness/bed approach reinforces the otherness of mental ill-health and people who experience it. Our thinking has not really evolved from the Victorian 'out of sight out of mind' mentality and the inherent dangerousness we associate with mental illness.

Financial arrangements

In England in particular, but also across the UK, our financial systems are not designed to accomplish the systemic change needed. In particular there are three financial factors that actively discourage progressive practice:

- payments based on service activity, not positive outcomes

- year on year budgets that discourage spending now even if it yields substantial savings later

- fragmented budgets spread across health, social care, criminal justice, housing and so on.

Complicated and fragmented

This last point highlights one of the biggest practical problems with trying to implement a whole community approach: the number of different agencies and budgets that would need to work together in order to achieve the necessary integration and responsiveness. The Welsh adoption of Local Partnership Boards and holistic care and treatment planning are positive steps in the right direction, and emerging processes in health payment systems in England are at least acknowledging these difficulties, but much more would need to be done to enable the wholesale changes required.

Bringing together whole communities and preparing communities for their role in a Lille approach is a major piece of work. It was not done well during the closure of the long-stay hospitals and it is hardly being done at all now. Interesting work is being done on dementia-friendly communities, and that may offer a model that mental health can adopt.

But some bits already work here, and others could…

Despite these challenges, it is worth noting that elements of the Lille approach are already happening here, and others would not take miracles to achieve.

Host families

Hertfordshire Partnership, an NHS Foundation Trust, has been running a family host service since 2010, which was supported by knowledge from the experiences of the service in Lille. The award-winning service is recognised as a progressive alternative to hospital admission, and it could be replicated elsewhere in the UK.

Using art and culture as a mechanism for social inclusion

The role of art in UK communities is not as familiar as it is in France (or Italy, where the philosophy originated), but there could easily be analogous mechanisms that are appropriate as a community focus for inclusion. Beyond mental health, sport, reading, music, dance, cooking and even horticulture are used by communities to foster broader involvement and engagement. Although art was fundamental to Trieste and Lille, there is no reason why any activity which has meaning to broader communities could not be used as the focus or catalyst for social inclusion.

Regular cross service conference calls

So many problems occur when people move between services or get stuck for a long time in the wrong service. Adopting regular cross-service meetings, held either physically or virtually, could produce significant dividends. Whole system thinking may be very difficult to achieve, but communication between services and beyond has never been technically easier or more cost-effective. There is no excuse for the silo working that characterises much of what goes wrong in services today.

Conclusion

It is more than 50 years since Franco Basaglia set out a genuinely radical way of working with mental ill-health. Much of what he proposed would still be considered radical today. The services in Lille embody the true spirit of that philosophy in a way that is hard to find anywhere in the UK (or even Europe).

The UK remains fixed on arguments about insufficient bed numbers and, despite adopting the language of empowerment and equality, we still seem to be led by service priorities and treatment delivery rather than whole community approaches for whole community issues. The services in Lille are not perfect, nor are they a quick fix or overnight solution, but they provide a concrete example of what can be done in the real world with imagination, commitment and a long-term view.

Acknowledgements

This chapter would not have been possible without support from Jean-Luc Roelandt and Laurent Defromont (Lille, France) and Ewan Hilton (UK).

References

Roelandt JL, Daumerie N, Defromont L, Caria A, Bastow P & Kishore J (2014) Community mental health service: an experience from the East Lille, France. *Journal of Mental Health and Human Behaviour* **19** (1) 10–18.

Scheper-Hughes N & Lovell AM (Eds) (1987) *Psychiatry Inside Out: Selected writings of Franco Basaglia* (trans AMLovell & T Shtob). New York: Columbia University Press.

Torrey EF & Yolken RH (2009) Psychiatric genocide: Nazi attempts to eradicate schizophrenia. *Schizophrenia Bulletin* **36** (1) 26–32.